P9-ARZ-641

JUVENILE JUSTICE

A Reference Handbook

Other Titles in ABC-CLIO's
CONTEMPORARY
WORLD ISSUES
Series

Books in the Contemporary World Issues series address vital issues in today's society such as genetic engineering, pollution, and biodiversity. Written by professional writers, scholars, and nonacademic experts, these books are authoritative, clearly written, up to date, and objective. They provide a good starting point for research by high school and college students, scholars, and general readers as well as by legislators, businesspeople, activists, and others.

Each book, carefully organized and easy to use, contains an overview of the subject, a detailed chronology, biographical sketches, facts and data and/or documents and other primary-source material, a directory of organizations and agencies, annotated lists of print and nonprint resources, and an index.

Readers of books in the Contemporary World Issues series will find the information they need in order to have a better understanding of the social, political, environmental, and economic issues facing the world today.

JUVENILE JUSTICE

A Reference Handbook

Donald J. Shoemaker
Timothy W. Wolfe

with the assistance of
Danielle McDonald

**CONTEMPORARY
WORLD ISSUES**

A B C C L I O

Santa Barbara, California
Denver, Colorado
Oxford, England

Library of Congress Cataloging-in-Publication Data

Shoemaker, Donald J.
    Juvenile justice : a reference handbook / Donald J. Shoemaker and Timothy W. Wolfe.
        p.   cm.—(Contemporary world issues)
    Includes bibliographical references and index.
    ISBN 1–57607–641–5 (hardback : alk. paper)—ISBN 1–57607–642–3 (ebook) 1. Juvenile justice, Administration of—United States—Handbooks, manuals, etc. I. Wolfe, Timothy W. II. Title. III. Series.
HV9104.S448 2005
364.36'0973—dc22

                                                                   2005019813

09   08   07   06   05   10 9 8 7 6 5 4 3 2 1

This book is also available on the World Wide Web as an eBook.
Visit abc-clio.com for details.

Production Team
    Acquisitions Editor: Alicia Merritt
    Production Editor: Cisca Schreefel
    Editorial Assistant: Alisha Martinez
    Production Manager: Don Schmidt
    Manufacturing Coordinator: George Smyser

ABC-CLIO, Inc.
130 Cremona Drive, P.O. Box 1911
Santa Barbara, California 93116-1911

This book is printed on acid-free paper ∞.
Manufactured in the United States of America.

To our wives, Beth and Doria,
and to juvenile justice workers
everywhere.

Contents

Preface and Acknowledgments

Juvenile delinquency is a topic that has interested the public and academic scholars for decades. When hearing the word "delinquent," most people think of street gangs or bands of teens running loose and frightening people in streets or parks. However, delinquency covers a range of behaviors from minor offenses, such as trespassing, to the more serious crimes often associated with gangs.

Because of the many different kinds of behaviors that constitute delinquency, public reaction to youth misbehavior is often mixed. On the one hand, there is a lenient attitude expressed toward youthful offenders, an attitude that is often expressed in the philosophy and operation of juvenile courts and throughout the juvenile justice system. Sometimes, however, juvenile crimes are too serious and threatening to respond to with lenience. In these instances, there are provisions within all state legal codes to transfer juvenile cases to the adult courts. Once a juvenile case has been transferred to the adult system, if convicted, the juvenile stands to be punished for his or her crime by the same measures used for adults, with the exception of the death penalty. Thus, in these cases, youth are no longer viewed as youth but, rather, as young adults.

The purpose of this book is to provide an overview of delinquency and the juvenile justice system in the United States. Historical and contemporary ideas, major historical events, and important legal cases will be discussed. Programs and individual contributions to the historical development of juvenile justice, the undersanding of youth misbehaviors, and societal responses to such behavior will be discussed as well.

It is hoped that by reading this book, one will have a firmer understanding of the historical antecedents of the contemporary juvenile justice system, the complexities of understanding and dealing with the full range of delinquent behaviors, and a better appreciation for the efforts of public and private citizens and organizations to understand and manage youthful offending.

As with any book, the completion of the project involves the assistance and cooperation of many people. In particular, we would like to thank the professional staff at ABC-CLIO, especially Alicia Merritt, for their continued assistance and guidance throughout the production of this book as it took many turns and encountered numerous delays. In addition, we would like to recognize the helpful assistance of our secretarial staff, particularly Dianne Marshall. We would also like to express appreciation to Jason Milne and Jeffrey Toussaint, graduate students in the Department of Sociology at Virginia Tech, for their contributions to earlier versions of the manuscript. We would especially like to recognize the invaluable efforts of Danielle McDonald at Indiana University of Pennsylvania who contributed important and indispensable information to several chapters of the book. Lastly we would like to express appreciation to our families, especially Beth and Doria, for their unfailing support and encouragement throughout this process.

Donald J. Shoemaker
Timothy W. Wolfe

1

The Development of Juvenile Justice in the United States

I n the fall of 2002, people in the mid-Atlantic states, especially Maryland and Virginia, were terrified by an increasing number of shootings of children and adults. There appeared to be no pattern to the killings, as young and old, men and women were shot down in parking lots, gas stations, and other public locations. Investigators were certain that a serial killer was on the loose, and they tried to determine one of a number of profiles they thought fit the killer. After weeks of mounting fear and terror, the killer was caught sleeping in a car at a rest stop in Maryland. However, it turned out that there was not just one murderer, but two, and one of them happened to be a juvenile.

The case of Lee Boyd Malvo and John Allen Muhammad is probably one of the most notable serial killer cases in U.S. history. The case involved several states, plus the federal government. One of the murdered victims was an analyst for the FBI, and several incidents occurred in the Washington, D.C., area. In addition, the case involved an adult who supposedly influenced the motivations and behavior of a juvenile. However, later investigations indicate a far different picture of the young man than was initially presented. Lee Boyd Malvo was seventeen years old during the time of the killings and may have not been as easily influenced as was once thought to be the case. In fact, some of his purported statements indicate that he initiated some of the shootings.

This case is also illustrative of how older adolescents accused of serious crimes are handled in the United States. That is, they are often waived or transferred to the adult court system. Furthermore, in Virginia, as in many other states, juveniles who are at least sixteen years old when they committed a crime can be given the death penalty if convicted of the crime in an adult court. This is one of the reasons—and perhaps the major reason—why the Malvo case was ultimately handled in Virginia. Because of the emotionally charged nature of the crime, the case was transferred from Manassas, Virginia, to Chesapeake, Virginia, where in December 2003, Malvo was convicted of murder. That same jury recommended that Malvo be given a sentence of life in prison with no possibility of parole instead of the death penalty. In March 2004, the presiding judge accepted the recommendation of the jury.

In March 2005, the U.S. Supreme Court banned the death penalty for juveniles who were under the age of eighteen when they committed the crime (see Chapter 5). Prosecutors in the Malvo case are now reconsidering filing additional charges against Malvo. Their thinking is that if the Court rules that juveniles cannot be given the death penalty, as it did, further prosecution of Malvo would be pointless and a waste of taxpayers' money, since prosecutions for capital cases can be expensive. (As an aside, Malvo's companion in the case, John Allen Muhammad, was convicted of capital murder and sentenced to death.)

The Malvo case is one of many involving juveniles tried in the adult system that come to the attention of the public almost every year. For example, there is the case of Jon Romano, a sixteen-year-old who shot and wounded his special-education teacher in Maryland, in February 2004. Another celebrated case involves a twelve-year-old male, Lionel Tate, who was accused and convicted of killing a six-year-old girl in 1999 in his home in Florida. At that time, Tate was one of the youngest defendants in modern times convicted of a crime in an adult court. He was given a term of life in prison, but the conviction was overturned in January 2004. Tate subsequently pleaded guilty to a charge of second-degree murder in connection with the crime in exchange for a three-year sentence in a juvenile facility, which he had already served; 1,000 hours of community service; a year of house arrest, to be relaxed only for limited reasons, such as for school and church; counseling and psychological testing; and ten years of probation.

In addition to these cases, there have been several recent school shootings involving juveniles, including the one at Columbine High School in Colorado in 1998. On September 24, 2003, for example, a freshman high school student in a small town in Minnesota shot and killed a classmate and wounded one other student during school hours. The causes of these incidents are numerous, but the fact that they occur demands our attention as we attempt to predict and hopefully prevent future occurrences of violence and crime in our nation's schools.

The purpose of this book is not to discuss various explanations for school shootings, drug use, or delinquency in general but rather to discuss the ways in which society handles cases such as those mentioned above, as well as the many other cases of crime and delinquency, both major and minor offenses, that occur every year. In essence, we will talk about the juvenile justice system in the United States in its historical and contemporary contexts. In so doing, we will show the reader how cases are processed through the system, and we will provide key terms used in the juvenile system and how they differ from the adult system. We will also present contemporary statistical data on juvenile delinquency and the juvenile justice system. We will then provide contemporary information on the sources of data and information concerning juvenile offenders and efforts to deal with and/or prevent delinquency, including Web sites created for this purpose. The present chapter, as well as Chapters 3 and 4, attempt to detail many of the key figures and events that led to the development of the juvenile justice system in the United States. Other chapters will address more contemporary data, events, and influential figures, including the Malvo and Muhammad case.

Problems with juveniles have existed for ages. As William Sanders demonstrates (1970), juvenile offenders have been breaking the laws and rules of society for at least 1,000 years, and we could probably extend this time frame thousands of years more. Societies have never truly solved their problems with the younger generation, and most likely, a solution will never be found. It seems as if every generation feels its way of doing things is better than that of the current set of young people. Still, it would be incorrect to say we have not learned some useful ideas about how to manage the growth and development of our youth over the years. For example, if we are to believe our magazines and newspapers, although injuries to children and sexual abuse of the young still exist, child abuse is becoming less common, and child abusers are subject to punishment more often. In addition, community-based programs such as alternative schools and the Boys & Girls Clubs, established for troubled young people, are much more common than they were a couple of generations ago.

We must remember that juveniles are the province of all of us, and no particular governmental agency or voluntary organization will have the ultimate answer on how best to handle juvenile offenders. However, it is important to know what others have done in the past and what is being done currently if we are going to better our efforts to reduce crime and delinquency in our society.

The Development of Childhood

According to Empey (1982, 71), the modern conception of childhood began to appear in the sixteenth and seventeenth centuries. Before this time, infancy lasted until about the age of seven, at which point individuals were considered adults (Elkin and Handel 1989, 22–23). Juveniles, especially during the Middle Ages (roughly 500 to 1500), were considered as responsible for their actions as were adults. They could be executed for their crimes and were not accorded special status because of their age.

The experience of childhood was often difficult. Children were often abandoned or simply killed, with few, if any, penalties given to their parents. Children of wealthier parents were often given to a wet nurse for caregiving and rearing. During these times, the practice of swaddling, or tightly wrapping babies, was common. The practice was thought to have many advantages, including cleanliness, but it also allowed caregivers to leave infants on their own while adults went about their daily business. Many now believe that swaddling actually increased health risks to the infant and probably contributed to high rates of infant mortality (Empey, Stafford, and Hay 1999, 20–22; Siegel and Senna 2000, 14).

By the time children were seven or eight, their clothing was replaced with adult-style garb. Even the playing of childlike games was restricted to the first few years of life. As Aries claims, by the time a child was five years old, the games that were played were the same as those for adults (Aries 1962, 50–61, 71). Indeed, the lives of young people during these times were harsh and, compared to life expectancy in modern society, considerably short. For example, in the 1600s, children in England could expect to live to about the age of thirty, while over half of children died before the age of twenty. These same harsh, short living conditions also existed in the early American colonies (Empey, Stafford, and Hay 1999, 22–23).

This adultlike treatment was given to all youth, rich or poor. Even children of European royalty were not spared adult jokes and sexual behavior. As a child, the future King Louis XIII, for example, was fondled and kidded in sexual ways, to the raucous amusement of his caregivers and members of the court (Empey, Stafford, and Hay 1999, 23).

In Europe, as children aged, again whether they were rich or poor, they were often apprenticed to craftsmen or businessmen, under conditions that treated them as if they were little adults. This condition was also part of early colonial life in America. Some children found their way to America through contracts, which bound them as apprentices to ship owners, craftsmen, and proprietors of business ventures for several years (Empey, Stafford, and Hay 1999, 23–24).

The adult status of young people was also reflected in the laws and the system of punishment for crimes. English common law, for example, maintains that a person becomes legally responsible for his or her actions at the age of seven, when "infancy" passes (Adler, Mueller, and Laufer 2001, 276). Juvenile delinquency, as we know the concept today, did not exist in those times. We know that during medieval times, seven was the age at which a child was considered capable of understanding speech, and this was probably why seven was selected as the age at which children became criminally responsible for their actions (Postman 1982). It is likely that seven was also regarded as the age at which people were able to reason the consequences of their actions, and thus children seven years and older were held accountable for their criminal behavior.

Even though English common law saw seven-year-old children as able to reason the consequence of their actions, it also provided that persons aged seven to fourteen were not as fully responsible as adults and were thus granted reduced punishment for their criminal actions. Yet social historians have found that adult-type penalties, including the death penalty, were applied to children throughout the Middle Ages, as well as during colonial times and into the twentieth century in the United States. Many colonial laws were influenced by Puritan beliefs and the high degree of respect for familial structures stressed by these Puritan beliefs. In colonial times, for example, a Massachusetts law permitted the death penalty for children aged sixteen years and above who disobeyed their parents! On closer inspection, there is no record of disobedient children ever actually being executed for such disobedience, but the fact that this penalty was possible tells us what Puritan and other colonial lawmakers felt about the place of children in society (Sanders 1970).

The concept of childhood and the special status that is associated with this position are recent developments. Some, such as Neil Postman (1982, chaps. 2 and 3), argue that the concept of childhood started to develop in the fifteenth century, when the printing press was developed. The invention of the printing press made reading possible for the common person. Postman suggests that the invention of the printing press gave society a firm basis for distinguishing when a person was able to understand the laws and policies of society. The establishment of the printing press meant that a person could begin to develop some literacy. Since it would take years to learn to read, becoming literate meant an accomplishment that signaled the readiness of a person to accept responsibility for actions that might offend societal rules and laws.

Others, however, suggest that societal awareness of childhood emerged in Europe and the United States gradually over several centuries, beginning with the Renaissance, and continuing through several social eras, culminating with the Industrial Revolution (Empey, Stafford, and Hay 1999, 25). People became increasingly aware that children needed to be emotionally and physically nurtured, as well as nourished, and that attaining adult status took several years to accomplish. Many dedicated citizens contributed significantly to the increasing awareness of the developmental needs of children and thus to the creation of the concept of childhood (Empey, Stafford, and Hay 1999, 25). In Chapter 4, we will discuss many of these individuals and their contributions to the societal awareness of children and, ultimately, to the development of the contemporary juvenile justice system in the United States.

The gradual transition of the definition of childhood from miniature adulthood to a special developmental period was characterized by backward steps as well as forward motions. While many manuals and policies were developed in response to the increasing recognition of the protected status of childhood, other philosophies were being advanced that effectively returned children to their miniature adult status, especially in the eyes of the law.

A prominent philosophical and, ultimately, legal idea was expressed in Cesare Beccaria's 1764 treatise *On Crimes and Punishment*. Beccaria was a young Italian scholar in his mid-twenties who had training and education in a variety of subjects, such as mathematics, economics, and philosophy. He was also interested in social justice. He decided to write this treatise at a time when penalties for crimes, at least in most parts of Europe, were determined by judges, not by elected representatives of the public. These judges were handing out sentences that were often random and would suit the judge's own views of punishment, not the views of the common people. Consequently, one man might receive a light sentence for a crime such as robbery, while another convicted criminal might receive the death penalty or a long prison term for the same crime.

Beccaria believed this situation was unfair. He argued that differential treatment would result in less respect for law and order rather than more respect for the rule of law. According to Beccaria, all people, regardless of age, are able to judge the consequences of their actions. In addition, all people act in accordance with free will, meaning that individuals have complete control over their actions. Therefore, all people should be subject to punishment for their criminal behavior. According to this line of reasoning, punishing offenders would be the best way to stop crime. However, Beccaria also believed that certainty of punishment was more effective in controlling crime than severity of punishment. Certainty of punishment meant that it was better to administer some kind of punishment to an offender, even if it meant reducing the punishment. In fact, if a punishment was harsher than social justice would suggest, it might create less respect for the law that established a particular act as a crime. For example, if petty theft were to be punished by death or a very long prison term, that might create confusion and eventually disrespect on the part of the public for the laws and penalty structures in a society.

These ideas and other notions formulated by Beccaria are now referred to as the classical school of thought in criminology.

They are associated with punishment for criminal behavior, but it is punishment that is not connected with the circumstances of the crime or with the situation of the criminal. Because of the view that all people, regardless of age or mental ability, are to be subject to the same penalties for a crime—that is, punishments should be based on the crime, not the criminal—it is sometimes the case that injustice results. For example, if a very young person, who does not understand the consequences of her or his actions as much as an adult would, is convicted of a serious crime and sentenced to a long prison term, that would be considered an injustice to some. Many would feel that the young person should be given a chance to redeem himself or herself. In addition, it is questionable whether the mentally disabled or mentally ill should be punished for their actions to the same extent that we punish the mentally competent for their criminal behavior. Today, we in the United States are seeing evidence of this kind of thinking when we see many states and courts passing laws and judgments that eliminate the death penalty for mentally disabled criminals.

Not only did the philosophy of the classical school contradict the common law doctrine that seven should be the minimum age for criminal responsibility, it also sent the message that childhood was not a special status for extra consideration in the eyes of the law. Despite this contradiction, Beccaria's ideas were highly regarded in Europe for many years, especially in those countries influenced by Roman law. Roman law did not accept the principles of English common law, so it is not surprising that some European countries more easily accepted the notions of the classical school than did England and its colonies. For example, most of Beccaria's ideas were incorporated into the French Penal Code of 1791. Eventually, however, that code was revised, in part because of the difficulty in establishing clear evidence of a guilty mind (to be discussed later) in young people, as well as in people of reduced mental capacity (Vold, Bernard, and Snipes 1998, 21–22).

In the place of such a rigid view of human behavior there has emerged in Western legal systems a whole set of conditions and circumstances that reduce, and sometimes eliminate entirely, individual responsibility for criminal actions. In the United States, for example, circumstances that reduce punishment for criminal responsibility include intoxication, physical illness (such as taking pain medications), emotional and physical abuse, fear of being harmed, and many other conditions. An important factor in the reduction of punishment is the offender's age. In addition to the English common law proscription of charging anyone under the age of seven with a criminal offense, there exists an entire set of laws, policies, and procedures recognizing that personal accountability should be reduced because of age. For example, people under age eighteen are handled within the juvenile justice system, where there are special conditions for serious crimes and judicial processing procedures, which will be discussed in Chapter 2. Sometimes, this age is lower than eighteen. For example, the age of sixteen is the maximum age of jurisdiction for juvenile courts in Georgia, Illinois, Louisiana, and five other states, while in Connecticut, New York, and North Carolina, the maximum age of juvenile court jurisdiction is fifteen. (Jurisdiction refers to the domain in which authorities have the right to prosecute an offender.) Usually, however, seventeen is the maximum age at which a juvenile case will be handled within the juvenile justice system.

Once a person reaches the age of eighteen, the juvenile court loses original jurisdiction over any criminal charges filed against that individual. We say "original jurisdiction," because in most states, if a juvenile is in the juvenile justice system during the time he or she attains adulthood, then the courts may retain jurisdiction over that individual until the age of twenty-one. Say, for example, that John Doe was arrested and referred to juvenile court for the crime of arson when he was seventeen years old. Assume also that John was found delinquent by a juvenile court judge and placed on two years' probation. If John reoffended after he turned eighteen but before his probation period was finished, he may still be kept under the jurisdiction of the juvenile court system until the age of twenty-one.

This additional three-year period of jurisdiction exists because originally the age of majority was twenty-one. The passage of the Twenty-Sixth Amendment of the U.S. Constitution in 1971 changed the age of majority (the right to vote) to eighteen. Until then, many states had allowed the juvenile justice system to continue jurisdiction of juveniles until the age of twenty-one. It is not clear why this discrepancy in age and legal jurisdiction remains. Perhaps it is because we are reluctant to consider eighteen-year-olds fully responsible for their actions. For example, in Virginia, as in many other states, it is illegal for a person under the age of eighteen to purchase or possess tobacco products. However, it is illegal for a person under the age of twenty-one to purchase or possess alcoholic beverages. In this case, the state is separating status offenses—offenses for which only juveniles are punishable; for example, running away—by age. Although the juvenile court or the juvenile justice system may not often retain juveniles who reach age eighteen, it can occur.

In addition, all states also allow for the transfer, or waiver, of juveniles to the adult court system. If a child is charged with a particularly violent or dangerous crime, such as rape or murder, and if the crime was committed when the child was a certain minimum age, usually age fourteen or fifteen, then the child can be transferred to an adult court. Essentially, what happens in the case of a transfer or waiver is that the juvenile charged with a crime will be subject to a trial in a criminal court instead of a hearing in a juvenile court. Many states are revising their laws and procedures for transfer, mostly making it easier for transfers to occur. The reader should keep in mind, however, that a juvenile convicted of a crime within the criminal justice system may face the death penalty or incarceration with older inmates.

In the latter situation, if the juvenile is ultimately released from prison, what would be the chances of that person starting over? What may we expect a child to have learned in prison, sharing the same facilities with more hardened adult prisoners? There may well come a time, in the not-too-distant future, when states will begin to rethink the wisdom of charging more and more juveniles as adults and change their laws accordingly, making it harder to send a juvenile case to the adult criminal justice system. The issue of waivers or transfers is complicated, and we will discuss it in more detail in Chapter 5 of this book.

Despite the influence of Beccaria in the eighteenth century, the special needs and care of children began to be recognized in postmedieval Europe. For example, poor laws started to appear in Great Britain in the middle of the sixteenth century. The first poor law was passed in England in 1535 (Siegel and Welsh, 2005, 10). Basically, poor laws allowed the government to send poor children to the homes of prosperous, or at least moderately successful, businessmen, craftsmen, and so forth. These children could be forced to stay with that family until they became adults. The hope was that they would learn the skills or crafts from the heads of these families, but there is very little evidence that this actually occurred. While these laws essentially reinforced the apprentice system, they also had the effect of providing some amount of welfare for poor and destitute children.

Another consequence of these poor laws was that the welfare might have permanently separated a child from his or her own family. In addition, not all poor children were placed with good families; some were sent to poorhouses or other places of work, and, of course, some were left to roam the streets unsupervised and without the assurance of daily food or permanent shelter. Furthermore, we can assume that not all placements in the homes of the affluent were successful—the members of the family may not have been able to get along with the youth—and the child may have been forced to leave. In other cases, there simply may not have been any suitable homes available for the youngster.

In the seventeenth and eighteenth centuries, manuals and essays began to appear that tried to establish more formally what being a child meant. From these treatises, the concept of an ideal child emerged. These ideals included five principles: supervision, discipline, modesty, diligence, and obedience (Empey, Stafford, and Hay 1999, 26). The ideal child was to be closely watched, self-controlled, and well mannered. The child was never allowed to discuss, let alone see, sexual matters, especially involving the opposite sex. Children were required to work hard and be obedient to adults (recalling the old adage that children are to be seen and not heard). While some of these ideas may have existed for several centuries, their enunciation began to crystallize the new meaning of childhood in ways never accomplished before.

In summary, it is clear that through the Middle Ages, Western societies typically viewed children as little adults and treated them in an adultlike manner. They were dressed as adults, played adult games, and were held criminally responsible for their actions. Gradually, over the course of several centuries and through the efforts of many intellectuals, philosophers, and policy makers, changes in the conceptualization of childhood and adulthood began to emerge. In modern society, in most Western nations and in developing countries as well, there are numerous child advocacy groups and organizations, some over 100 years old. There are also juvenile justice systems in almost every society and on every habitable continent of the world (Shoemaker 1996). The connection between the conceptualization of childhood and the development of juvenile justice systems is no coincidence. The following section describes the earlier processes and events that helped shape the current system of juvenile justice in the United States. While this discussion concentrates on the United States, there were many international contributions to the U.S. juvenile justice system, especially from Great Britain. The U.S. juvenile justice system now has incorporated so much international influence from various countries, such as intervention and prevention programs aimed at juvenile populations, that it is incorrect to say that the system represents just one country.

Juvenile Justice in the United States: The Beginnings

The history of juvenile justice in the United States can be summarized into several periods. Bartollas (2000, 12–20) divides the development of juvenile justice into the following periods: the Colonial Period (1636–1823); the House of Refuge Period (1824–1898); the Juvenile Court Period (1899–1966); the Juvenile Rights Period (1967–1975); the Reform Agenda of the Late 1970s; the Social Control Period, or "get tough" era, of the 1980s; and a continuation of the get tough era in the 1990s. Of course, these periods contain considerable overlap and, in reality, cannot so easily be confined to specific years. In addition, it is clear that juvenile justice policies are not as clear-cut as these divisions suggest. Bernard (1992), for example, makes a good case for describing juvenile justice policies and procedures in terms of cycles. In one time period, he sees evidence of treatment, or rehabilitative policies, while in another period, there are clear signs of control or punitive policies. Then, the pendulum swings back to another period of treatment or rehabilitation. Again, these shifts are not automatic, nor always clear-cut. But we can describe trends in the juvenile justice in general terms, such as rehabilitation or punishment, and not be misleading in doing so.

The history of juvenile justice in the United States does not begin solely within the borders of this country. Before the nineteenth century, especially in Europe, many institutions housed juveniles, either exclusively or, more often, alongside adults. In England, for example, Bridewell prisons, or houses of correction, were established in the 1500s to house beggars and vagrants, in essence operating as a debtors' prison. These institutions held adults and children alike. The full purpose of these institutions is not clear. While they almost certainly had some rehabilitative function, they were also used to simply warehouse youngsters until someone claimed them or they grew too old to stay in the institutions. In 1704, Pope Clement XI built the Ospizio di San Michele, or Hospice of St. Michael, in Rome. This hospice actually served as a type of correctional prison for youth under twenty who were deemed incorrigible or idle and in need of correctional discipline and religious instruction (Drowns and Hess 1995, 13).

Separate institutions established exclusively for housing juveniles or young adults are a relatively recent development. Even more recent is the creation of a separate system of juvenile justice, consisting of not only correctional institutions but also separate juvenile courts, or hearings for juveniles, rehabilitation programs, and probation programs, to mention just a few components of the juvenile justice system. The need for special treatment of juveniles was not significantly recognized until the early part of the nineteenth century, particularly in the United States. The events and new ideas that led to the creation of special institutions for juveniles and, ultimately, to an entirely separate system of juvenile justice, largely occurred throughout the nineteenth century. Some refer to these activities and legislative actions as the child-saving movement. This movement reached a significant milestone with the passage of the first delinquency law, and accompanying juvenile justice concepts, in 1899.

Many significant achievements in the child-saving movement were the result of the efforts of what Anthony Platt (1977) and others have called the "child savers." Child savers were men and women who labored to create and maintain legal and social systems that would nurture and reform juvenile offenders. Many of these individuals were philanthropists, often middle- and upper-middle-class women who worked for several decades to ensure the passage of laws and procedures that would better protect the interests and welfare of children.

The welfare of children was considered a concern of women in particular. The stereotypes of women in the nineteenth century were based around the model of a housewife and mother. One of the child savers, Louise Bowen, once suggested that women were entitled to influence matters dealing with the home and family, such as trash collection and neighborhood conditions, and the education of the young, since the place for women was supposed to be in the home. Furthermore, an administrator of the State Industrial School for Girls in Michigan remarked that a "reformatory without a woman" was "like a home without a mother—a place of desolation. In reformatory work, the woman (sic) is the good mother. The pulse of the school or home throbs in her breast. She is the one to whom all look for comfort and relief'" (cited in Platt 1977, 79). Some of the child savers' efforts can be traced to the early nineteenth century, but most of their activity was concentrated in the second half of the nineteenth century.

Child savers were rightly concerned about the welfare of children and young adults. Some critics believed, however, that the child savers' efforts were directed more toward preserving standards of living and lifestyles among the middle class, especially middle-class whites, than toward protecting the safety and welfare of children. Although some of the child savers may have been patronizing, many of them seemed to have genuine interest and concern for the poor and disadvantaged. The rest of this chapter describes many significant events of the nineteenth century that contributed to the development of the juvenile justice system, particularly in the United States, as we know it today.

Houses of Refuge

The first institution built to house troubled juveniles and juvenile offenders, was the New York House of Refuge, which opened in 1825. It was established by a group of philanthropists who in 1817 formed the Society for the Prevention of Pauperism (SPP), which in 1824 became known as the Society for the Reformation of Juvenile Delinquents (Krisberg, 2005, 26-27). The members of the SPP embarked on a campaign of social reform for poor and mostly immigrant families, including children, throughout New York. Included in their agenda for reform were poverty and its associated problems, such as vagrancy, gambling, prostitution, and public drunkenness. Some argue that these early reformists were interested in preserving the values and lifestyles of the more privileged members of society, namely middle- and upper-middle-class whites.

Whatever the real motives of the SPP, houses of refuge became very popular throughout most of the eastern seaboard and in other regions as well, particularly the Midwest. Soon after the New York House of Refuge was established, similar institutions were opened in Boston and Philadelphia (Grossberg 2002, 16-18). By the 1840s, there were over fifty such institutions scattered throughout the East Coast and the Midwest. Most served male populations and some could accommodate as many as 1,000 inmates (Bartollas 2000, 518). In part, these institutions were developed to treat juvenile offenders because more traditional ways of dealing with juveniles—such as keeping them with their families or having them serve apprenticeships—were not working. According to one Virginia publication, for example, the "utter Rewing (ruin) and undoing" of an apprentice was due to the negligence of his family (Mennel 1973, xxii). Moreover, apprentices were being taken on merely for the value of their labor, not to be taught the values of learning a trade or, more important, how to work. A growing number of apprentices were fleeing their masters and getting into trouble on the streets because they had no homes and no one to supervise their activities.

Houses of refuge were designed to handle not only juvenile offenders but also young people with behavioral problems, such as running away, rebelliousness, and vagrancy, which at that time were not illegal acts. It was assumed that disciplining young people who exhibited these behaviors would change them for the good, despite the lack of any civil or legal rights accorded to the institutionalized (Empey, Stafford, and Hay 1999, 40). During this time, there were no published accounts of what actually happened to those youngsters who were sent to houses of refuge. Scientific methods for studying human behavior and social institutions were not generally recognized among scholars and reformers. Consequently, no one really knew with certainty whether these institutions actually worked; that is, whether the youth released from their doors were rehabilitated and therefore committed fewer delinquent acts as a result of their confinement.

Despite the lack of hard evidence that houses of refuge reclaimed lost lives and put young people back on the right track, early supporters envisioned that offenders would benefit from an extended incarceration. Administrators of these institutions believed that a lack of education and proper training were significant causes of juvenile criminality. They strived to educate these young people through strict discipline, hard work, and the loving care of substitute parents. Substitute parents were needed because the natural parents were deemed incapable of properly rearing their own children. Most of these inmates were from lower social classes and immigrant populations. Moreover, the earliest institutions maintained a strict racial segregation policy consistent with mores of the late nineteenth century. Black juveniles were placed in separate, segregated facilities, such as the House of Refuge for Colored Juvenile Delinquents, which opened in 1848 in Philadelphia, or in a separate wing of a white house of refuge, such as the addition constructed at the New York House of Refuge in 1834. Economic diversity and racial or ethnic harmony were not the goals of houses of refuge or of other juvenile institutions (Mennel 1973, 17–18).

In addition to the values of hard work and discipline, houses of refuge were also supposed to teach their residents some sort of practical trade that could be used to obtain regular employment and pay. Another dominant view of delinquency at the time was that poverty was a cause of crime. Because most of the inmates in these houses of refuge were populated by those who were poor, it was accepted that criminals, young or old, typically came from lower-class or immigrant families. Poverty, or pauperism, was considered the root cause not only of delinquency but also of many other negative social conditions, such as intemperance (drinking) and gambling.

To underscore the idea that youth sent to houses of refuge needed discipline and control in their lives—the kind of values missing from their natural families—the schedule for these institutions was rigid. Order and routine were important to the administrators of these institutions. Typically, the inmate's day began around daybreak, when the youth had to make his or her own bed. This was followed by a lockstep march to the washroom. After washing up, the children were marched to the courtyard, where they underwent inspection for cleanliness. After prayer, school began at 7:00 A.M. A while later, the children were marched to breakfast, then to workshops until lunch at noon. After lunch, they worked again until 5:00 P.M. From 5:00 to 5:30, they had supper, followed by more school until 8:00 P.M. Breaks during the daily schedule were often signaled by the ringing of a bell. After evening studies were completed, there was another prayer session, followed by confinement to the dorm rooms, where inmates were supposed to maintain strict silence until daybreak. The schedule was more relaxed on holidays and Sundays. (Rothman 1971, chap. 9, especially pp. 221–225; Mennel 1973, 18–19). Residents who disobeyed the rules or failed to follow the rigid schedule were often punished with whippings or physical restraints.

Young people were often sent to these institutions for behavior that was not strictly criminal, and for the most part, they had no legal protections or safeguards whatsoever. Robert Mennel states that "of the first sixteen children admitted to the New York House of Refuge, nine had not committed a punishable offense" (1973, 13). Most of the early inmates of the New York House of Refuge had not committed a crime but were characterized by idleness, vagrancy, or similarly undesirable characteristics.

Houses of refuge were established by both private, philanthropic groups and governmental agencies. The backers of these institutions were often from rich and powerful families. In New York, for example, the House of Refuge was supported by industrialists. Religious faiths, such as the Quaker, Methodist, and Episcopalian churches, had also become very involved with prison reform in the eighteenth and nineteenth centuries. The juveniles were sent to houses of refuge by court order; not by juvenile court judges, however, for juvenile courts did not exist at that time, but by adult criminal court judges. These judges were often persuaded by the rich and powerful people backing prison reform. These same rich and powerful people wanted to build new institutions for juvenile offenders, institutions such as houses of refuge, in order to separate the delinquent individuals from society. And these same people made it clear who they thought should be housed in these institutions. These youth were not their own sons and daughters, but the children of the lower and immigrant classes. Consequently, the parents of the children sent to houses of refuge had to accept what had happened to their children, or they had to find some way to fight their cases in the courts, an avenue of opportunity that was not commonly made available to lower- and immigrant-class parents. Some, perhaps many, of these parents were not even citizens of the country.

Of course, many children confined to houses of refuge resisted the restraints and punishment handed out by the directors. Many tried to escape. Mennel (1973, 29–30) estimates that between 1839–1841 in the New York House of Refuge, almost 40 percent of the inmates tried to run away.

Not all of the parents of these inmates were willing to accept society's judgment of their child-rearing abilities. Many lower- and immigrant-class parents of inmates strongly objected to the incarceration of their child for noncriminal reasons, not to mention the denial of legal rights to the inmates. One of these objections reached the Supreme Court of Pennsylvania, resulting in a momentous ruling that affected the development of juvenile justice reforms for decades to come. In this case, known as *Ex Parte Crouse* (1839), the court ruled that the state of Pennsylvania was within its rights to place a child in a house of refuge, even though she had not committed a crime, because the girl was being treated, not punished. In reaching this decision, the court evoked the legal doctrine of *parens patriae*. Basically, this doctrine allows the state to do whatever it sees fit for a child, as long as such actions are in the best interests of the child (Siegel and Senna 2000, 17–20).

Parens patriae (Latin for "father of his country") is a legal doctrine that was created in England several hundred years ago. It was part of the chancery court system, which dealt with civil matters and issues concerning families and children. Originally, the term meant that children and property (children were considered the property of their parents at that time) belonged to the king; thus, the king is the father of the country. As it was adapted in the colonies, *parens patriae* was changed to reflect the interests of the state rather than the monarchy. An early court case in England, *Wellesley v. Wellesley* (1827), for example, permitted the king to take a child of the royal family away from him for unfit behavior (Siegel and Senna 2000, 17–18).

Today, *parens patriae* is considered the legal backbone of the juvenile justice system. It has withstood many tests of constitutionality and is still used to allow juvenile courts and other juvenile justice agencies the authority to remove children from the care and custody of their parents and even to deny parents contact with their children if it is considered by the state to be in the best interests of the child to do so.

The power of *parens patriae* should not be underestimated. It allows representatives of the state (and local communities as well), to do whatever they deem appropriate with a juvenile offender, as long as this is done in the best interests of the child. For example, directors of a juvenile institution have the right to refuse parental visitation if they think such visits would be harmful to the child or to the institution. They can even monitor communication between inmates and parents, or anyone else who might want to contact a child in an institution.

Not allowing institutional officials to monitor communication between inmates and their friends or relatives can have dangerous consequences. In a juvenile institution where one of the authors of this book worked many years ago, one of the inmates had read a letter from a relative that had not been screened by the staff. The author of the letter had apparently disowned the child for the behavior that had resulted in incarceration. After throwing the letter to the ground, the child ran to the top of a water tower and threatened to jump. Quick thinking and calm, level-headed responses from the institution's staff kept the youth from jumping off the water tower, over fifty feet high, to certain injury or death. While institutional authorities may seem to be controlling and distrustful to screen and monitor inmates' communication, not doing so may cause greater harm to youth and their caregivers.

Despite the outcome of the *Crouse* case, the popularity of houses of refuge began to decline around the middle of the nineteenth century. By that time, however, the idea that juveniles needed separate confinement, apart from adults, and that children needed to be nurtured rather than hardened had become more commonly accepted. In 1853, for example, the Children's Aid Society was formed in New York City, largely with the support of William Brace. One of the central assumptions of this organization was that children need the nurturing and protective presence of a wholesome family in order to develop to their full potential. To accomplish these objectives, the society first wanted wayward children to be removed from the streets. Consequently, the Children's Aid Society advocated the temporary placement of abandoned, neglected, and criminal children into stable homes that would encourage good child development (Grossberg 2002, 19–21). This practice is considered the forerunner to the modern concept of foster homes (Siegel and Senna 2000, 439). The Children's Aid Society also helped develop institutions for more permanent placement of wayward youth found on the streets of New York. One such facility was the Newsboys' Lodging House (Grossberg 2002, 20).

Later, in the middle to late 1800s, the notion of the temporary placement of children in local homes and institutions expanded to include more permanent placement of such children into homes in rural areas. This practice was known as "placing out" (Empey, Stafford, and Hay 1999, 40). Trains were often used to transport street children and other youth from their home cities to these distant locations. In time, they became known as "orphan trains." In a discussion of the early years of child-saving organizations and practices in the United States, Michael

Grossberg maintains that for a quarter of a century, from 1854 to around 1880, "orphan trains removed more than fifty thousand children from New York" (2002, 20).

Eventually, the ideas and procedures of Brace and the Children's Aid Society met with resistance. Some claimed that the children who were placed out were often not given proper care and attention in their new homes. Others, such as the leaders of the Catholic Church, charged Brace and the Children's Aid Society with anti-Catholicism, arguing that many of the youth so placed were from Catholic families and backgrounds and that Brace and his followers were Protestants interested in converting Catholic youth to the Protestant faith (Grossberg 2002).

Despite these claims and criticisms, the Children's Aid Society in New York spread to other cities throughout the latter half of the nineteenth century. The idea of private organizational assistance in resolving the problem of street youth and wayward children seemed to have been accepted by many Americans, even though governmental efforts and public institutions were still being used and were expanded well into the twentieth century (Grossberg 2002, 21–38).

Training Schools, or Reformatories

While houses of refuge and placing out eventually disappeared from the juvenile reform landscape, there appeared a more enduring feature of juvenile justice, starting around the middle of the nineteenth century. The more permanent fixture for handling problem youth was known as a training school, or reformatory. The first state-supported reformatory was established in Massachusetts in 1846. Early on, a hallmark feature of such institutions was the use of the cottage system (Siegel and Senna, 2000, 630).

The cottage system first appeared in female reformatories but soon became the prototype for juvenile institutions in general. The child savers who influenced these early models of juvenile reformatories argued that the cottage system was better adapted to establish a family-like setting for young children. In particular, cottages with a female leader would be optimal settings for rehabilitation. (Most reformatories were used for housing younger adolescents, not the very young.)

The system is based on placing several small cottages within a compound. Each cottage can house two to three dozen juveniles, and each is supposed to be headed by cottage parents (Siegel and Senna 2000, 630). These facilities were thus conceptualized as replacements for the natural family, although in an institutional setting.

The cottage system is an interesting feature of juvenile correctional facilities that does not occur in adult prisons. The cottage house essentially becomes the central focus of the inmate's life inside the institution. This is where the inmate sleeps, studies, watches television, reads, and relaxes. Often the structure of the cottages resembles a boarding house. A typical arrangement is a three-part ranch-style residence. On one side is the dormitory-style sleeping quarters for the inmates, large enough to accommodate approximately thirty juveniles. Sleeping cots or daybeds are arranged along the walls of the room. In cases of overcrowding, the institution directors might have to put more than thirty youth in one room, in which case double bunk beds are used or inmates sleep on cots placed in the middle of the room. In the middle of the structure is a day room, where the inmates and staff congregate during the day to play recreational games, watch television, study, and so on. In the third wing of the cottage are the living quarters of the cottage parents. This is often little more than an efficiency apartment, with a small kitchen, a den, a bedroom, and a bathroom.

The cottage parents are not parents as such; because married couples are hard to find, sometimes the parents are single men or women. Often the director of the institution is forced to hire college students, or people in between jobs, either as temporary replacements or as full-time employees. Ideally, the cottage parents would be a married couple, preferably a couple with grown children. In practice, however, few institutions have been able to maintain a true cottage system with an intact couple heading the cottage year-round. However, an institution is not a family, no matter how hard we may try to make a correctional setting into a family, families are not organizations and vice versa.

Despite some of the difficulties and organizational problems associated with the use of cottages as places for the treatment and rehabilitation of juvenile offenders, the idea of treatment remained strong in the minds and philosophies of child savers and others who wanted to change the system of justice and corrections for young people. Their activities helped pave the way for the eventual appearance of delinquency laws and the formulation of juvenile justice as it is known today. Reformatories and other correctional institutions are now a regular component of juvenile justice systems in most of the country. However, the cottage system, which was a regular feature of older institutions, is still found in some institutions.

Although reformatories are a common element of the U.S. juvenile justice system, the utility and cost of such institutions is often a subject of debate. Private institutions can cost over $45,000 per child per year. To put one child into a public institutional facility can cost more than $30,000 per inmate, on average (Bartollas 2003, 511). In addition, there are many different models of reformatories, with different names applied to them, such as "learning centers," a term formerly used in Virginia, or "correctional institutions," the name currently used in Virginia. Some are based on a wilderness type of experience and have no fences around their grounds.

Whatever the name or expressed purpose of such facilities, they are all places of incarceration and custody. Since the majority of the inhabitants do not enter the facilities voluntarily, these places are also coercive institutions. Sociologist Erving Goffman is credited with coining the term *total institutions* to refer to such facilities (Goffman 1961) since they are expected to fulfill almost all of an inmate's daily needs, including educational and medical requirements. Correctional institutions are bureaucratic in organizational format and are usually operated on a standardized plan or schedule. Rather than treating each child individually, then, the institutional structure forces, or at least encourages, directors and staff members to place common rules and restrictions on all of the inmates so that the whole operation can run more smoothly.

Often the result of these total institutions and strict bureaucracy is a child whose sense of self changes. A total institution that is confined within a strict bureaucratic sense may produce a child who becomes one of the crowd. Since there are so many children living in these institutions and since the institutions are often headed by only a few people, the ratio of children to staff members is high. The result is a lack of individualized attention, love, and care that can be given to a child. So while these institutions have tried to simulate the family structure, because of the strict bureaucracy and control over every part of the child's life, such a family structure may not be possible.

The first such institutions were also called "industrial schools." Industrial schools were much like what their name indicated. They were prisons, of course, but they were also places where juveniles were trained to work at some type of job or occupation when they were released from the institution. These jobs almost always involved manual labor or minimal skills training. Rarely, if ever, would juvenile reformatory inmates be given a college-level education or professional training.

Most reformatories or training schools were able to house about 100 inmates; some of these institutions, however, were very large. The physical structures were imposing, built mostly of brick and mortar, especially during the latter half of the nineteenth century, and the juveniles sent there might expect to remain in the institution until they were in their late teens or early twenties. The length of stay for each inmate was open; that is, inmates were not given specific sentences. Instead, they were committed to the institution by a judge for an unspecified period of time. They were to be released when the director of the institution felt they were ready to be released.

Child Savers and Other Nineteenth-Century Juvenile Justice Reform Efforts

Because of the Civil War, the 1860s saw little in the way of juvenile reform. We can assume that young troublemakers were sent to battle arenas or at least joined the Confederate or Union armies. However, in the 1870s, many significant events occurred that changed the direction and shape of juvenile justice, even into modern times. One of these events was an 1870 Illinois Supreme Court case known as *People ex rel. O'Connell v. Turner*, which involved a young man who had been committed to the Chicago Reform School on the grounds of vagrancy and "misfortune." The Illinois Supreme Court validated a lower court's decision, asserting, in essence, that confinement of juveniles on the grounds of noncriminal acts such as "misfortune" was unconstitutional (Siegel and Senna 2000, 438, 441).

Not only did the *O'Connell* decision change the reformatory movement in Illinois, but it also had an impact on juvenile justice reform throughout the country. While many child savers had been working for various reforms before 1870, after the *O'Connell* case, they now had a definite goal to achieve. Most important was the passage of new legislation and policies that would allow children to be removed from their homes and placed into various institutions for treatment, discipline, hard work, or whatever the directors of the institution wished the children to receive. Thus, according to Anthony Platt (1977), the reformatory movement began in Chicago in the 1870s, although some argue that it began earlier in the century, with the establishment of organizations focused on children's welfare and the creation of houses of refuge.

Many of the child savers in the latter part of the nineteenth century, like those before them in the early 1800s, were wealthy housewives, who had education and political connections to assist in the achievement of their goals (Platt 1977). The contributions of these women and their colleagues to the welfare of children cannot be denied, and some of them will be discussed in other sections of this book. However, the upper-middle-class background of the child savers has led some to question the purely moralistic motives of their efforts. Rather, these critics suggest that these reformers sought to control immigrant and poor children and protect middle-class values and policies (Siegel and Senna 2000, 437). That very few, if any, of the children taken from their parents and placed in institutions were from upper-middle-class homes lends support to this view. In fact, the social backgrounds of most inmates in public juvenile institutions today is still dominated by youth from lower- and working-class families. The social class differences between those who are in institutions and those who are not is another issue of the U.S. juvenile justice system, an issue that will be discussed more fully in Chapter 5.

Despite the contemporary critical view of the child savers, it cannot be denied that treatment of children was one of their main goals. The emphasis on treatment developed gradually, as most social change does. However, in 1870, the National Prison Congress held its first meeting in Cincinnati. One of the accomplishments of the meeting was the passage of principles to govern the use of institutions. One such principle was that prisoners, young or old, should be treated while in prison and that prison terms should be indeterminate; that is, not fixed, but dependent upon the inmates' behavior and progress in treatment. Thus, a central theme at this meeting was the education and reform of prisoners in the United States, especially young prisoners. The efforts of those attending this congress had a significant impact on the ways in which juvenile institutions were operated for the next several decades. Additionally, the philosophy of a new juvenile justice system was developed and spearheaded by the upper-middle-class reformers based in Chicago. Future prisons and reformatories would reflect the congress's message of rehabilitation, reform, open-ended sentences, and the like for many years to come (Platt 1977, chap. 3). The first prison to be established following the principles of the Cincinnati Prison Congress was a reformatory built in Elmira, New York, and administered by Zebulon Brockway (Platt 1977, chap. 3). Elmira Reformatory was not created solely for juveniles, but more so for teenagers and younger adults, some aged thirty to forty. Brockway was considered an enlightened prison administrator. He took many of his ideas not only from the Prison Congress but also from prison systems established earlier in England and Ireland. A central feature of the Elmira Reformatory was a graded system of incarceration based upon the principle of indeterminate sentences. Every inmate entered the system at Grade 2, which was a middle ground. This grade level typically lasted for about six months. If the inmate successfully completed Grade 2, the next phase was Grade 1, which also lasted about six months. Successful completion of Grade 1 allowed the inmate to be considered for parole.

Parole is similar to probation, in that the offender lives in the community but has to follow certain rules while under the watch and supervision of a parole officer. An important difference between probation and parole is that probation is used for convicted offenders before they are sent to a prison or reformatory, while parole is used for inmates who have been released from prison. If inmates at Elmira successfully completed the period of parole, they were released from prison custody. However, if at either Grade 2 or Grade 1, or presumably during the parole period, the inmate disobeyed authority figures or failed to follow prison rules, the consequences would be placement in Grade 3, which lasted a minimum of one month. After one month of good behavior, the inmate was eligible for promotion to Grade 2, and then the process started all over again (Barnes and Teeters 1959). This system became a model for many reformatories established in the late nineteenth and early twentieth centuries. The graded system of confinement is also an early system of behavior modification, which is used in several detention centers and juvenile correctional institutions today in the United States. In 1874, the Society for the Prevention of Cruelty to Children (SPCC) was formed in New York City, and by the end of the century, many other such organizations had been established. One of the SPCC's main functions was to influence legislative bodies to pass laws and regulations that helped protect abused and neglected children, homeless youth, and otherwise at-risk youngsters, especially those from underprivileged backgrounds (Siegel and Senna 2000, 440–441).

The efforts of the child savers resulted in the passage of the Illinois Juvenile Court Act in 1899. This law, which for the most part covered Chicago, established for the first time the legal status of delinquency, including what is popularly known today as a status offense. As mentioned earlier, a status offense is an act that is illegal only because of a person's age, especially when the offender is younger than eighteen. The Illinois Juvenile Court Act, though, established the age of majority at sixteen. For status offenses, the law does not usually stipulate that a crime has occurred. Rather, it is assumed that a juvenile has committed an act that is a sign of other troubles and that the behavior should be corrected before it leads to more serious trouble. Examples of such acts included begging, selling things and/or playing musical instruments on the street (for children under eight years of age), and associating with disreputable people. A child who was dependent (that is, without parental or guardian support and in need of public support), neglected, or abandoned was also cause for police or court intervention, because such conditions were thought to lead to criminal activity (Siegel and Senna 2000, 442–443).

Today, examples of such illegal acts for children include running away, disobeying parental orders, skipping school, and possession of alcoholic beverages. However, status offenses have typically included a wide assortment of activities, including cases of abandonment and abuse, which allow the courts to intervene on behalf of the best interests of children, even when no law has been broken (Teitelbaum 2002). Sometimes, state legislatures can be creative in their selection of activities to outlaw for juveniles. In Indiana, for example, status offenses used to include "wandering at night" and " being found near trains or trucks" (Dineen 1974, 36). Many of these statutes focused on sexual activity and child-parent relationships, such as disobeying lawful rules and orders of parents. For this reason, status offenses have sometimes been referred to as "omnibus laws" because they can be extremely far-reaching and so inclusive as to cover virtually anything a child might do. So loosely worded are these laws that they would probably not stand up to tests of constitutionality if they applied to adults.

The Illinois Juvenile Court Act also created other institutions and procedures that had a major impact on juvenile justice. For example, the act created the first separate juvenile court for counties that had 500,00 people or more. In addition, it introduced probation officers into the court, to whom juveniles may be assigned for supervision and treatment. The act also allowed adults in the community, including nonrelatives of juveniles, to petition the court to hear a charge of delinquency against any juvenile in the community. The belief behind the ruling was that the community had a responsibility to supervise the child, not just the child's parents or guardians. All of these provisions were meant to be in the youngster's best interests and were created to help, not punish, wayward youth. Punishment for juvenile offenders was becoming secondary to the goal of treatment and prevention for delinquents. Juveniles under the age of twelve were not to be placed in jails, and youth under the age of ten were not to be committed to reformatories or other places of confinement (Siegel and Senna, 2000, 442–443).

By 1917, all but three states had passed similar legislation. These juvenile court laws classified juveniles as offenders separate from adults and stressed the need for treatment and preventive measures for juvenile offenders as opposed to punishment (Platt 1977, 10; Siegel and Senna 2000, 442–445). The legitimacy of these laws seemed to be firmly established in another court case. In 1905, the Pennsylvania Supreme Court ruled, in *Commonwealth v. Fisher,* that state juvenile courts had the right, through the legal doctrine of *parens patriae,* to remove children from their homes and to do whatever else was necessary to protect the community and children (Siegel and Senna 2000, 438). One effect of this ruling was that it encouraged other delinquency laws as well as other policies and procedures relevant to the processing of juveniles through the state courts and correctional systems.

Despite the seemingly revolutionary impact of the Illinois Juvenile Court Act, things did not go as smoothly for the child savers as they had hoped after the law was passed. For example, suitable institutions for handling the new kind of juvenile offender had to be developed. In addition, alternative arrangements for treatment or some kind of supervision had to be developed, especially since very young children could not be placed into correctional institutions or jails at all. Funds for these new facilities and treatment programs were not readily available from the state or the city of Chicago. Initially, the new law and the system of juvenile justice that was to come on its heels were not universally accepted; it was resisted by politicians, prosecutors, judges, and administrators of institutions. Eventually, money for creating new institutions and programs had to be provided largely through private donations and fund-raisings. Thus, many of the child-saving advocates had to remain vigilant in overseeing the new policies, programs, and procedures that were being created to deal with this new legislation. Prominent advocates in this vigilance were two early leaders of Hull-House in Chicago, Jane Addams and Louise Bowen, along with their friends and colleagues.

Today there are many protests against the wide-ranging, and potentially unconstitutional, powers of the court, and ultimately the juvenile justice system, over the rights and freedom of juveniles. However, several appellate cases decided in the early 1900s reaffirmed the constitutionality of these new laws and the powers of the courts to enforce them (Siegel and Senna 2000, 438).

Treatment Programs for Institutionalized Juvenile Offenders

In the nineteenth century, the image of the child began to change. Children were seen as not being as responsible for their actions as were adults. This alteration in the perception of youthful behavior had many influences. Policy makers and influential thinkers and movers of those times were instrumental in developing the notion that children were the products of their environment. Two themes in particular emerged from the laws, policies, and institutions that were established in the mid-nineteenth century: (1) urban, city influences were especially bad for the proper development of youth, especially areas populated by immigrant and foreign youth; (2) the family or, more properly, the breakdown of the family was behind much of the criminal and miscreant behavior of young people, especially among those living in urban areas.

By the end of the nineteenth century, however, the view of delinquency had changed to what some call a medical model of behavior. In this view, delinquency is seen as a kind of symptom of an underlying illness. The focus of attention is on the juvenile, and the proper response to delinquency is treatment and rehabilitation. Early juvenile delinquency laws, including the first delinquency law in 1899, were characterized by the notion that today's delinquent is tomorrow's criminal. Thus, it was considered important to identify troubling behaviors in young people, especially status offenses, in order better to treat, correct, or otherwise alter these behavior patterns and change the young delinquent into a law-abiding citizen before it became too late. Child-guidance clinics were often established in connection with juvenile courts in order to work with troubled youth on a more individualized basis (Krisberg 2005, 41–44).

A popular psychological theory to emerge during this time was psychoanalytic theory. Psychoanalytic theory is most often identified with the writings and thoughts of Sigmund Freud (1920), but the field was also developed by many other psychologists and psychoanalysts, such as Freud's own daughter, Anna Freud (1935), August Aichhorn (1925), and William Healy and Augusta Bronner (1936), to name a few.

A central feature of psychoanalytic theory, as applied to delinquency, is the notion that our personalities develop in stages of growth, especially stages of sexual development, and that events can happen during these stages, particularly in preadolescence, that can significantly affect the development of our personalities. According to traditional psychoanalytic thinking, our personality is divided into three main components: the id, the ego, and the superego. The id is the part of our personality that involves impulses, urges, and instincts. For example, the id part of our personality tells us that when we are hungry, we need to control that hunger by eating. The id also tells us that these needs must be met immediately upon notice. The superego is the embodiment of societal views of morality and normative behavior. The ego is that component of our personality responsible for balancing the impulsiveness that can emerge from a dominant id against excessive fear, anxiety, and rigidity, which may reflect an overdeveloped superego. Thus, the ego is the control of both the id that makes us want to control all our needs immediately and the superego that says that we must follow society's rules completely. For example, when we experience hunger, we often try to curb it by eating. But we do not steal the food to satisfy the hunger; instead, we go to a store and buy it (Freud 1920).

Each of these three parts of the personality must be in balance and properly developed if our attitudes and behavior are to be within what are considered normal ranges. However, because of events during our developmental years, the relative balance of these three parts of our personality becomes altered and ultimately skewed. For Freud, often the things that happen are the result of overrepression or underrepression of our sexual urges. In some situations, a person whose personality has become dominated by the impulses and urges of the id may become overly aggressive and selfish. In other cases, an individual may develop a strong and rigid superego that may alter his or her perception of familial and other social relationships. For example, Sigmund Freud attributed the Oedipus complex, in which a boy imagines his father as a rival, sexually and socially, for his mother, to an ineffective superego (Freud 1920, 1927).

Psychoanalytic theory also embraces the notion that the experiences we receive in early life are too painful for our conscious, and thus we tend to repress them into our unconsciousness, or some would say our subconscious. Thus, in order to treat the outward manifestations of inner conflict, turmoil, and pain—in this case, delinquent behavior—the therapist must first make the patient aware of the existence of this inner pain and then recognize its source, which may be the real reason for the repression. All of this intensive analyzing not only takes time but also can be expensive. Consequently, the popularity of psychoanalytic theory as a source or basis for the treatment of delinquency began to fade, especially toward the middle of the twentieth century. In its place have emerged several other treatment strategies, based on different views of personality development and the impact of personality on behavior. Two examples of these newer theories—reality therapy and behavior modification—are discussed below. In Chapter 2, other treatment programs will be discussed, particularly those based on societal or environmental perspectives, and the use of behavior modification will be reexamined.

Reality therapy attempts to make juveniles more aware of the consequences of their actions and to be more responsible for their behavior. One result of this approach to the treatment of delinquents should be improved awareness of the consequences of one's actions and, ultimately, improved self-esteem and reduced delinquency. This approach to delinquency prevention was popularized by William Glasser in the 1960s (Glasser 1965), and it has seen some success in its application. As with most treatment programs that emphasize counseling and individualized attention, however, the success of this approach depends a great deal on the training and motivation of the counselor or treatment specialist (Siegel and Senna 2000, 644). Richard Rachin (1974) describes reality therapy as a response to the dissatisfaction with the traditional medical model, particularly psychotherapy inspired by psychoanalytic theory. According to Glasser and his supporters, such as Rachin, psychiatry should be concerned with meeting the basic needs of people, especially the need for love and the need to feel worthwhile (Rachin 1974, 49). Rachin (1974, 51–53) outlines fourteen specific steps involved in the treatment philosophy of reality therapy, most of which stresses present recognition and awareness of one's situation and consequences, good or bad, for behavior. Responsibility for one's actions is an important feature of reality therapy. In addition, reality therapy forces one to focus on realistic future plans for behavior and the need to address past tendencies and problems in developing more effective strategies and plans for future behaviors, especially those that involve rewarding consequences.

Behavior modification differs from other treatment programs in that it is based on the notion that to change a person's attitude, you must first change his or her behavior. In fact, the logic of this approach to delinquency is that changing behavior is the goal of treatment and rehabilitation in the first place. So it is acceptable if the attitude change does not occur but a change in behavior does occur. For example, if you are able to change an offender's bad behavior but not the attitude that promotes or accompanies that behavior, at least you have changed the behavior; that is, the danger or problem to society.

Behavior modification programs are influenced by the theory of differential reinforcement proposed by C. Ray Jeffery (1965). Jeffery argues that if behavior is punished, it is less likely to occur. Similarly, if a behavior is rewarded, it is more likely to occur. The goal of behavior modification is to reward those behaviors that the administrators want the inmates to engage in and to punish those behaviors that the administrators are trying to deter. As the name indicates, the goal is to reinforce the good behavior with positive actions and to deter bad behavior with punishment.

Behavior modification programs have been most successful in tightly controlled settings, such as juvenile correctional institutions. In these places, such programs often take on the character of merit systems or reward-and-punishment systems. In more elaborate examples, juveniles are placed into categories of behavioral units, sometimes living together in separate dormitories or cottages. When the individual or group exhibits the appropriate amount of good behavior, they are transferred to another living unit. Eventually, they are released with some type of supervision, usually juvenile parole or aftercare.

The advantage of behavior modification programs is that they can change a person's behavior patterns while the person is in custody or in the treatment program. The disadvantage of these programs is that changes may not be long lasting, especially if the juvenile is released back into the same environment that helped produce delinquency in the first place. In fact, studies have shown that unless the behavior is continually reinforced, people will often revert to the old behaviors once they return to society. Thus, a return to crime is often possible. The return to crime after being released from an institution or going through a treatment program is called recidivism. Recidivism rates can be particularly high for drug offenders, partly because of their addiction, but also because of the nature of the environment where the addiction and drug-using habits were formed. The return to old habits is another indication that we need to pay attention to the social factors that contribute to delinquency, and not only to individual personalities.

Contemporary Organizations, Programs, and Developments

In 1860, the first Boys Club was established in Hartford, Connecticut. In 1906, the national Federation of Boys Clubs was created in Boston, with fifty-three member clubs. In 1990, the name of the club changed to Boys & Girls Clubs of America (B&GCA). Today, there are over 3,300 Boys & Girls Clubs throughout the United States, serving the needs of more than 3 million youth. In 1994, the headquarters of the organization was moved to Atlanta, Georgia. The B&GCA receives support from many private individual and corporate sources. In 2002, its level of financial support exceeded $100 million. Boys & Girls Clubs try to identify at-risk youth and work with them in their schools and neighborhoods, showing them ways to become successful adults and moving them away from destructive, criminal, and delinquent activities. B&GCA sponsors dozens of activities in schools and neighborhoods throughout the country, but some long-standing programs include the Keystone Club and the Torch Club, which focus on developing leadership and civic-mindedness among young teens. More recently, B&GCA has developed a gang prevention and intervention program called the Target Outreach Program, which attempts to identify youth who are at risk of becoming involved with gangs in their neighborhoods (Boys & Girls Clubs of America 2002 and other B&GCA literature).

In the second half of the twentieth century, legislatures and governmental agencies became more involved in the prevention and treatment of delinquency. Several laws and policies were established that further protected the rights of juveniles in juvenile justice proceedings. Perhaps the most far reaching of these laws was the federal Juvenile Justice and Delinquency Prevention (JJDP) Act of 1974, which provided millions of dollars to state juvenile justice agencies to modify their delinquency statutes and policies. At issue in most of the grants funded by this act was the elimination or revision of status offense laws and the provision of community-based programs to take the place of jails and institutions as places of treatment and rehabilitation for juvenile offenders. The law provided that by 1977 all states were to have modified or eliminated their status offense laws. Although that provision was relaxed somewhat the law did reduce the number of status offenders in our nation's jails and detention centers. The average daily population of juveniles in adult jails dropped from 12,000 in the 1980s to 2,000 in 1992 (Siegel and Senna 2000, 465). While we are not sure how many of these offenders were status offenders, it is reasonable to assume that many of those who were not imprisoned or detained were charged with status offenses. Of course, it is still possible for authorities to jail youthful status offenders if they are involved in some kind of criminal activity besides just running away or skipping school.

In addition to removing many juveniles from institutions and detention homes, the JJDP Act promoted other popular juvenile justice programs. One popular policy in juvenile justice is the practice of diversion. Diversion programs focus on the removal of youth from formal judicial intervention. In other words, their aim is to handle delinquent and at-risk youngsters in community-based settings, away from the attention of the courts and institutions.

Theoretically, diversion programs are based on the concept of labeling. Labeling theory argues that when people, either juveniles or adults, are arrested and sent through the formal system of justice, they are likely to become worse in terms of their attitudes and behaviors. This theory assumes that juveniles will start to become what they are labeled and will act the way they are treated. According to labeling theory, as juveniles are processed further into the juvenile justice system, they begin to receive additional labels that may be hard to shed once they are released from the system. Diverting offenders from courts and institutions, therefore, should result in less stigma and improved behavior. While evaluations of diversion programs do not consistently support these assumptions, such community-based efforts usually result in lower operating costs than are associated with institutional confinement (Siegel and Senna 2000, 522).

Since diversion programs essentially developed from governmental policies and laws, they have been evaluated in terms of results. These evaluations have demonstrated that one common effect of diversion programs is a phenomenon called "net widening." When net widening occurs, there are more juvenile offenders processed into the system than would have been the case if diversion had not been implemented. Some may argue that net widening is a good thing, since it means that more juveniles will receive some kind of treatment or help than they would otherwise receive. However, if the goal of diversion programs is to remove juveniles from the system, then net widening might be a sign of program failure. In addition, net widening might actually contribute to increased costs of diversion programs because the system would presumably have to handle more youth at greater costs than if fewer youngsters were being processed into the system (Bartollas 2003, 363–368). Despite these drawbacks, however, diversion programs are now a fixture of the larger system of treating and handling juvenile offenders, especially status offenders, and in large measure, this is the result of the JJDP Act.

In 1992, the JJDP Act was amended to include providing grants to communities attempting to create delinquency prevention programs. Throughout the 1990s, this program has helped more than 1,000 communities in the United States develop delinquency prevention programs (Siegel and Senna 2000, 464–465).

Juvenile Justice Today: A Return to Punitiveness?

A recent trend in the juvenile justice system has been the passage of more punitive legislation for juvenile offenders, including laws that promote increased waivers, or transfers, of juveniles from the juvenile court system to the adult criminal court system. There is no particular event or program that identifies this trend; rather, there are several legislative acts that collectively affirm this direction within juvenile justice. This trend is not confined to the United States. Other Western societies—nations such as Canada and Great Britain—are passing tougher laws for juvenile delinquents (Shoemaker 1996).

In the United States, the modern trend toward waiving juvenile cases to the adult criminal justice system began in the late 1980s and peaked in 1994. In that year, 12,100 delinquency cases were transferred to the adult system. In 1998, that number had decreased to 8,100, or less than 1 percent of all formal processed delinquency cases in that year (Puzzanchera 2001). In addition, some research on the effects of waivers suggests that those juveniles who are transferred to the adult court system have higher rates of recidivism when they are released than those who stayed within the juvenile justice system. It is not clear why the recidivism rate increases for those youth transferred to the adult system, but one reason may be that they are associating with more hardened offenders who are wiser about ways to commit crimes and ways to convince yourself that you will not be arrested. Another possible reason may be that the juvenile has now become labeled and is responding accordingly to that label by committing more criminal acts. These figures and findings might suggest that Americans are beginning to get soft on juvenile crime, or at least to rethink the wisdom of putting juvenile offenders into the same jails and prisons with adults. However, the use of waivers for juvenile offenders, especially for those charged with violent offenses and drug crimes, remains popular.

Countertrends to increasing punishment of juvenile offenders are the continued use of diversion programs as well as the growing use of restorative justice, which will be discussed in Chapter 2. Restorative justice programs are characterized by several models, but essentially they operate as alternatives to incarceration and are based on the idea of reconciliation and mediation between offenders and victims and others concerned with a case.

Despite diversion and restorative justice programs, it is difficult to identify a major shift away from increasing penalties for juvenile criminals. Rather, a more accurate conclusion might be that two models of juvenile justice have developed in the United States. On the one hand, for status offenders and juveniles not considered a threat to the community, there is a range of community-based alternative treatment and rehabilitative programs aimed at diverting youth from formal processing and being labeled as delinquent or criminal. On the other hand, for the more serious offenders, specifically those who are considered hardened or who have committed truly criminal acts, there is the possibility of transfer to the adult system or at least increased sentences within the juvenile system. In fact, both models of juvenile justice are at work simultaneously. As one author has observed (Bernard 1992), the cycle of more and more punishment is followed by another trend toward increased treatment and prevention for juvenile offenders, followed by another trend toward increased punishment, and this cycle has occurred several times. Neither trend seems to be dominant for a prolonged period of time. Consequently, these models of juvenile justice always seem to be overlapping, although for a short period of time one or the other may be relatively more popular.

Conclusion

The history of the treatment of juveniles has gone from a position of indifference and almost neglect to the creation of a special age of childhood, with care, treatment, and prevention as hallmark features. Along with this transition, there has occurred a major change in their legal status, from young adults, accompanied by a punitive philosophy, to young people who need special protection and consideration in the eyes of the law.

In the past few decades, there has been a call for a return to the more punitive philosophy that prevailed until the nineteenth and twentieth centuries. In effect, we are hearing from those who want a return to a previous time, when children were routinely punished for their bad behavior and were treated no differently from adults. This return to a former time, however, cannot easily be accomplished; from the turn of the twentieth century, there has developed an elaborate system of laws and procedures applying to people under the age of eighteen.

Despite the difficulties of returning to a former system, many states have passed laws that allow young people under the age of fourteen or fifteen to be sent to the adult court system for trial and punishment rather than to the juvenile court system for hearings and placements. This process of waiver or transfer has become a major challenge facing juvenile crime and the jurisdiction of the juvenile court today (Bartollas 2003, 451–455).

In addition, juvenile justice reforms are granting juveniles more legal rights, especially the right of legal representation from arrest through the court process. The renewed interest of the courts in the issue of juvenile rights reappeared in the 1960s and continues to the present. The 2002 Oklahoma case of *Board of Education of Independent School District No. 92 of Pottawatomie County et al. v. Earls et al.*, concerning drug testing of students involved in extracurricular activities, testifies to the continued interest of the U.S. Supreme Court in the rights of juveniles, not only in the juvenile justice system but in other settings as well, such as school systems. At the same time, many are advocating the transfer of juveniles to the adult system, especially for cases involving violence and drugs, although this process is still rarely used. In addition, laws are being passed that allow for more punishments for juvenile criminal offenders. Both of these trends seem likely to continue.

Issues of punishment versus treatment tend to assume importance in a cyclical pattern. At the moment it seems as if punishment is more dominant than treatment, although we have identified several programs and policies that seem to favor treatment over punishment. All of this could change in the next few years, and we could see a more intense effort at treatment over institutions and punishment than exists today. Despite the cyclical nature of policies and ideologies, however, the existence of a separate system of hearing cases and treating and punishing juveniles seems to be a permanent fixture within our legal and correctional systems. The U.S. juvenile justice system can no longer be considered an experiment that might someday disappear. Although it may be subject to modifications in the future, the basic system is here to stay.

Today, many policies and practices involving juveniles are considered more as civil matters than as criminal issues. Juveniles are committed to state correctional institutions rather than sentenced to prison terms. Technically speaking, juveniles are "taken into custody," rather than "arrested." We see this mixture of jurisdiction and philosophy concerning juveniles in situations where transfer or waiver to the adult court system is at stake. However, this kind of ambivalence regarding juvenile crime is at the heart of many other issues and disputes concerning the best methods of dealing with juvenile offenders. For example, should we give children the same legal rights in court as we give adults? Should we focus more on rehabilitation and less on punishment, regardless of the type of crime committed or the attitude of a youth charged with a serious crime? What effect does going through the juvenile justice system have on the child? In the next few chapters, we will discuss many of the important issues facing the juvenile justice system in the United States today, including waivers of juvenile offenders to the adult court system, the use of the death penalty for juveniles, challenges to status offense laws, and judicial reviews of juvenile justice concepts and practices.

References

Adler, Freda, Gerhard O.W. Mueller, and William Laufer. 2001. *Criminology and the Criminal Justice System*, 4th ed. New York: McGraw-Hill.

Aichhorn, August. 1925. *Wayward Youth*. Reprint 1965. New York: Viking.

Aries, Philippe. 1962. *Centuries of Childhood: A Social History of Family Life*. Translated from the French by Robert Baldick. New York: Vantage.

Barnes, Harry Elmer, and Negley Teeters. 1959. *New Horizons in Criminology*, 3rd ed. Englewood Cliffs, NJ: Prentice-Hall.

Bartollas, Clemens. 2000. *Juvenile Delinquency*, 5th ed. New York: Allyn and Bacon.

———. 2003. *Juvenile Delinquency*, 6th ed. New York: Allyn and Bacon.

Bernard, Thomas J. 1992. *The Cycle of Juvenile Justice*. New York: Oxford.

Boys & Girls Clubs of America. 2002. *Annual Report: It's About Time*. Atlanta: Boys & Girls Clubs of America.

Dineen, John. 1974. *Juvenile Court Organization and Status Offenses: A Statutory Profile*. Pittsburgh, PA: National Center for Juvenile Justice.

Drowns, Robert W., and Karen M. Hess. 1995. *Juvenile Justice,* 2nd ed. New York: West.

Elkin, Fredrick, and Gerald Handel. 1989. *The Child and Society,* 5th ed. New York: Random House.

Empey, Lamar T. 1982. *American Delinquency: Its Meaning and Construction,* rev. ed. Homewood, IL: Dorsey.

Empey, Lamar T., Mark C. Stafford, and Carter H. Hay. 1999. *American Delinquency: Its Meaning and Construction,* 4th ed. Boston: Wadsworth.

Freud, Anna. 1935. *Psycho-Analysis for Teachers and Parents.* New York: Emerson Books.

Freud, Sigmund. 1920. *General Introduction to Psycho-Analysis,* translated by Joan Riviere. New York: Liveright.

————. 1927. *The Ego and the Id,* translated by Joan Riviere. London: Hogarth.

Glasser, William. 1965. *Reality Therapy: A New Approach to Psychiatry.* New York: Harper & Row.

Goffman, Erving. 1961. *Asylums.* Garden City, NY: Doubleday/Anchor.

Grossberg, Michael. 2002. "Changing Conceptions of Child Welfare in the United States, 1820–1935." Pp. 3–41 in Margaret K. Rosenheim, Franklin E. Zimring, David S. Tanenhaus, and Bernardine Dohrn, eds., *A Century of Juvenile Justice.* Chicago: University of Chicago Press.

Healy, William, and Augusta F. Bronner. 1936. *New Light on Delinquency and Its Treatment.* New Haven: Yale University Press.

Jeffery, C. Ray. 1965. "Criminal Behavior and Learning Theory." *Journal of Criminal Law, Criminology and Political Science* 56: 294–300.

Krisberg, Barry. 2005. *Juvenile Justice: Redeeming Our Children.* Thousand Oaks, CA: Sage.

Mennel, Robert M. 1973. *Thorns & Thistles: Juvenile Delinquents in the United States, 1825–1940.* Hanover, NH: University Press of New England.

Platt, Anthony M. 1977. *Child Savers: The Invention of Delinquency,* 2nd ed., enlarged. Chicago: University of Chicago Press.

Postman, Neil. 1982. *The Disappearance of Childhood.* New York: Delacorte.

Puzzanchera, Charles. 2001. *Delinquency Cases Waived to Criminal Court, 1989–1998.* Washington, DC: U.S. Department of Justice.

Rachin, Richard L. 1974. "Reality Therapy: Helping People Help Themselves." *Crime and Delinquency* 20: 45–53.

Rothman, David J. 1971. *Discovery of the Asylum: Social Order and Disorder in the New Republic.* Boston: Little, Brown.

Sanders, Wiley, ed. 1970. *Juvenile Offenders for a Thousand Years: Selected Readings from Anglo-Saxon Times to 1900.* Chapel Hill: University of North Carolina Press.

Shoemaker, Donald J., ed. 1996. *International Handbook on Juvenile Justice.* Westport, CT: Greenwood.

Siegel, Larry J., and Joseph J. Senna. 2000. *Juvenile Delinquency: Theory, Practice, and Law,* 7th ed. Belmont, CA: Wadsworth.

Siegel, Larry J., and Brandon C. Welsh. 2005. *Juvenile Delinquency: The Core,* 2nd ed. Belmont, CA: Thomson / Wadsworth.

Teitlebaum, Lee. 2002. "Status Offenses and Status Offenders." Pp. 158–175 in Margaret K. Rosenbaum, Franklin E. Zimring, David S. Tanenhaus, and Bernardine Dohrn, eds., *A Century of Juvenile Justice.* Chicago: University of Chicago Press.

Vold, George B., Thomas J. Bernard, and Jeffrey B. Snipes. 1998. *Theoretical Criminology,* 4th ed. New York: Oxford.

2

The Contemporary U.S. Juvenile Justice System: Problems, Controversies, and Solutions

In this chapter, we address three primary topics. First, we examine the structure and procedures of juvenile justice. We look at its component parts and compare it to the adult criminal justice system. Second, we examine some of the more serious problems and controversies facing juvenile justice today. Third, we discuss several possible solutions to the problems identified. Before we take up these issues, several preliminary comments are in order.

It is important to recognize that the juvenile justice system—composed of law enforcement departments, the courts, corrections, and various family and child welfare agencies—does not exist in a vacuum. Instead, it is embedded within U.S. society; as such, it reflects the problems and worries, the strengths and weaknesses, and the uncertainties and contradictions of the wider culture. As an example, racism and discrimination have long been a part of U.S. social life. Therefore, it should not be surprising to hear claims that the juvenile justice system discriminates against certain racial groups. To what extent discrimination and racism exist is a matter of debate (and we will look at the various sides of the argument), but it would be foolish to think that there is none.

In addition, crime and delinquency have become highly politicized issues (Beckett and Sasson 2000). Today, politicians from both major parties compete to be judged tough on crime and delinquency. Candidates boast about their efforts to win the war on drugs and crime. Add to this situation the popular media's penchant for exaggerating and inaccurately portraying the reality of most crime and delinquency. It is really no wonder that myths about the nature and extent of delinquency persist. Decades of social scientific research have revealed some surprising findings:

- Crime and delinquency rates have decreased over the past decade.
- Drug use is lower today than it was twenty years ago (and certainly lower than it was 100 years ago).
- Most crime and delinquency are relatively minor in nature.*
- Schools are among the safest places for most young people.
- The U.S. crime rate, with the important exception of homicide, is average when compared to crime rates of other industrialized nations.
- Most young people—whatever their race, social class, gender, or other characteristics—are not involved in serious or violent delinquency.
- Images and stories that we get from politicians and the popular media are often inconsistent with social science research findings; problems are socially constructed by various claim makers to serve their particular interests.

We should also add that although the popular presentations of crime and delinquency are often distorted, real problems certainly do exist. Mass murders at schools and gang-related drive-by shootings are real occurrences. Children as young as ten or eleven do sometimes commit unspeakable acts of violence. Juveniles do indeed abuse drugs and alcohol, and some of them commit adult crimes. However, these problems should be viewed with a sense of perspective. That is, as citizens we need to put the problem of delinquency into a realistic framework so that we know how serious the problems are and what courses of action are most wise. Exaggerating or minimizing the various problems facing our communities is not helpful. We need to look carefully and honestly at the problems that we commonly lump under the heading of "delinquency" so that we can respond in the most efficient and just ways.

Recent trends in juvenile justice, however, suggest that the United States is not particularly inclined to look honestly at the problem of delinquency. Instead, it appears that we will continue with a narrowly focused punitive or "get tough" approach to dealing with troubled youngsters (Whitehead and Lab 1999, 394)—an obvious sea change from the original focus of U.S. juvenile justice (see Chapter 1). There is a tremendous tension between the original goals of juvenile justice (namely, helping young people in trouble) and the current cultural and political climates favoring accountability and punishment. Indeed, we believe that the biggest problem facing juvenile justice is this uncertainty of purpose, or what we call the "identity crisis" of juvenile justice.

We also think it is important to state at the outset that the problems facing juvenile justice, like most social problems, are many and complex. Thus, simple "commonsense" solutions (for example, boot camps and "scared straight" programs; see discussions that follow) and catchy slogans (such as "Old enough to do the crime, old enough to do the time") will not increase public safety, nor will such efforts improve the lives of juveniles, families, and communities. Along with many other observers of the juvenile justice system, we believe that what is needed is careful, systematic, and objective evaluations of existing programs and policies, especially some of the newer ones (University of Maryland 1997). Programs and policies that seem to work should be expanded, while those that do not should be modified or perhaps abandoned.

Furthermore, we believe that it is imperative that policy makers, juvenile justice practitioners, and concerned citizens recognize that delinquency has multiple causes. As James Garbarino (1999)—a leading expert in the field of delinquency prevention and treatment—has shown, simple X causes Y explanations of delinquency are misguided and ultimately not helpful in preventing and treating delinquent behavior. The clear trend among researchers and practitioners is to think of delinquency in more complex and holistic terms.

Will a child growing up in the inner city, surrounded by gangs, drugs, and guns, turn to a life of violence and wanton disregard for the welfare of others? It depends. Does the child's family have adequate resources (such as money, at least enough to cover basic living expenses, and enough time and energy to provide a reasonable level of adult supervision)? Do they use fair and consistent discipline (not too harsh, not too lenient)? Do the adults in the family act as good role models (for example, by not abusing drugs)? These things make a difference. Turning to delinquency depends on other factors too, ranging from the child's temperament to the economic conditions of the surrounding community (Garbarino 1999).

What does this mean for juvenile justice? Among other things, it means that responses (solutions) to delinquency must address multiple and complex causes if they are to be successful. We will look at possible solutions later in this chapter. First, however, we will present the structure and procedures that make up the juvenile justice system. We will also take a brief look at some of the differences between the juvenile justice and the adult criminal justice systems.

The Contemporary Juvenile Justice System

U.S. juvenile justice, though only a little more than 100 years old, is large, cumbersome, and confusing. What we call a "system" is composed of a multitude of agencies, both public and private. All fifty states have juvenile courts and juvenile correctional systems. Tens of thousands of people are employed by the various agencies and organizations, and hundreds of millions of dollars are spent annually on juvenile justice.

The primary components of the juvenile justice system include the police, the juvenile court, and juvenile corrections. We sometimes refer to these components as the "three Cs" of juvenile justice: cops, courts, and corrections. In addition to the three Cs, there are allied organizations and agencies—departments of social service and youth counseling centers, for example—that work with troubled youth and their families.

The number of cases that are handled by the various components of the juvenile justice system is tremendous. Each year in the United States, approximately 2 million juveniles are arrested by police; about half of these cases are formally petitioned (sent) to juvenile court; roughly 500,000 admissions are made to secured detention centers; and approximately 10,000 juvenile cases are waived or transferred to the adult criminal justice system (Siegel and Senna 2000). Boys are more likely to commit a delinquent offense than are girls, but the number of girls arrested has

Figure 2.1 Basic Juvenile Justice Case Flow

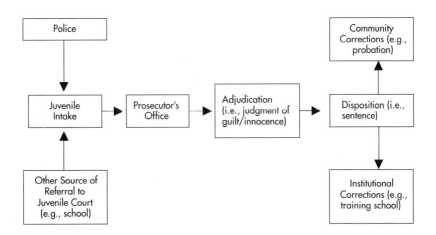

increased in recent years. In 1996, one in four juvenile arrests involved young girls (Office of Juvenile Justice and Delinquency Prevention 1999). Between 1990 and 1999, the rates of arrests for juvenile females increased at a much higher rate than those for juvenile males. For violent crimes, for example, the rate of arrest among juvenile females increased by 40 percent, whereas the rate of arrest among juvenile males increased by 11 percent (Siegel 2002, 32–33).

We can add to this the more than 3 million cases of suspected child abuse and neglect that are reported to child protective service agencies each year. As you can see, the system is inundated with cases.

Another way to look at the juvenile justice system is to examine the major steps or procedures that are involved from the time of arrest to release from the system. As Figure 2.1 shows, a youth typically enters the juvenile justice system via contact with law enforcement. Court procedures from initial intake to disposition (sentencing) comprise the second major step in the juvenile justice process. The final step involves juvenile corrections (for example, residential placement or probation). Each of these steps, in turn, contains many substeps. Another way to think about it is to consider the number of decision points that exist along the juvenile justice path—for example, arrest or release, re-

Table 2.1
Important U.S. Supreme Court Cases Affecting U.S. Juvenile Justice

Case (Year)	Ruling and Effect on Juvenile Justice
Kent v. U.S. (1966)	Established protection against transfer to adult court by imposing due process procedures on the court. Before a juvenile can be transferred, a hearing must be held, juvenile has a right to counsel, and juvenile and counsel must have access to social records.
In re Gault (1967)	Established that juveniles have basic due process rights (such as notice of charges, right to counsel, and privilege against self-incrimination).
In re Winship (1970)	Increased the standard or burden of proof from preponderance of evidence (relatively low standard of proof) to proof beyond a reasonable doubt (a much higher standard of proof) for juvenile adjudication proceedings.
McKeiver v. PA (1971)	Denied juveniles the right to a jury trial (although some jurisdictions now allow this). This case had the effect of reminding observers of the juvenile justice system that although juveniles have certain constitutional rights and protections, the juvenile justice system is still separate and distinct from the adult criminal justice system.
Breed v. Jones (1975)	Established that Fifth Amendment protection against double jeopardy (being tried twice for same offense) applies to juveniles. Juveniles cannot be tried in juvenile court and later in adult court for the same offense.

fer to court or handle informally, detain or release back into the community, place on probation or remand to a secure or lockup facility, and so on.

Juvenile justice in the United States increasingly resembles the adult criminal justice system. Whereas the original founders of the juvenile court wanted to avoid the formal and legalistic trappings of the criminal justice system, for several decades, especially since the 1960s, we have witnessed a movement to make the juvenile justice system more formal and more legalistic. The U.S. Supreme Court has often led the way with a number of important rulings, some dating back to the nineteenth century; several such cases and rulings are presented later in this chapter. However, a few cases have particularly affected the rights of juveniles in the court system; some of these are presented in Table 2.1.

Table 2.2
Key Differences between U.S. Juvenile Justice
and Criminal Justice Systems

JUVENILE SYSTEM	CRIMINAL JUSTICE SYSTEM
Juveniles are "taken into custody"	Adults are "arrested"
Juveniles are "adjudicated delinquent"	Adults are "found guilty"
Juveniles are "committed" or "placed"	Adults are "incarcerated"
Juveniles have no right to jury trial	Adults have right to jury trial
Juveniles have a right to treatment	Adults have no right to treatment
Juvenile proceedings are generally informal	Adult proceedings are formal
Status offenses apply	Status offenses do not apply
Identifying information not released by courts	Courts must release information
Death penalty not applicable	Death penalty applicable
Juvenile record sealed	Adult record is permanent

As a result of these Supreme Court rulings, plus several other cases, the juvenile justice system increasingly resembles the adult criminal justice system in many respects. However, there are important differences between the two systems. Table 2.2 presents some of the key differences in terminology and procedures for juveniles and adults.

As Table 2.2 makes clear, there are many important differences between the juvenile and criminal justice systems. Not only is the terminology different (for example, "committed" for juveniles versus "incarcerated" for adults), but juveniles generally receive more treatment and protection, while adults receive more punishment and fewer rehabilitation efforts. These differing conditions, of course, were the intent of the founders of the juvenile justice system. Even though the juvenile system is becoming more like the adult system, obvious differences remain. This duality of justice—one for juveniles and one for adults—is an example of the "identity crisis" that exists today in juvenile justice. Do we uphold the ideals of the founders, or do we abandon their goals and treat juveniles like adults?

Problems and Controversies

A number of difficult juvenile justice issues are being debated today. At what age should a juvenile be tried and sentenced as an adult? What treatment and rehabilitative efforts, if any, actually work for juvenile offenders? Do boot camps and other military-type programs reduce recidivism; that is, a return to crime or delinquency? Are programs based on a philosophy known as restorative justice (see discussion later in the chapter) the way to go? Should the juvenile court continue to have jurisdiction over both delinquents and status offenders? What rights do juveniles have in juvenile court? Should we simply abandon the juvenile justice system?

In addition to these questions, many people have raised other provocative and perplexing concerns: Why are minorities overrepresented at various stages of the juvenile justice process? Do poor and minority youth actually commit more crime, or are they victims of a discriminatory system?

Concern over the misbehavior of youngsters is not at all new. As long as there have been adults and children, there have been concerns and complaints about bad behavior. The founding of the first juvenile court in the United States occurred only a little more than a century ago. So while concerns about youthful miscreants are age-old, a formal and separate system of justice for juveniles is relatively new. Interestingly and perhaps ironically, many of the dilemmas faced by the founders of the juvenile court are dilemmas we still face today (Cox and Conrad 1996, 9).

What is typically called the juvenile justice "system" is far more complex, complicated, confusing, and confounding than the term itself would suggest. The various components of the system often fail to work efficiently and effectively with one another (Inciardi 2002). So what is called a system may be something more like a nonsystem. As one delinquency researcher plainly puts it (Bartollas 1997, 557), "[T]he juvenile justice system is chaotic."

The juvenile justice system, especially the courts, can be confusing and intimidating to parents and youth alike (Hubner and Wolfson 1996). As juvenile justice professionals and researchers who have spent many hours in juvenile court and in juvenile correctional facilities, even we, the authors of this book, have found the system to be at times confusing and intimidating. One can easily imagine the confusion and intimidation faced by people with no background in juvenile justice.

In addition to the problem of chaos or system disarray, there is the related problem of system overload. That is, increases in juvenile delinquency and referrals to the juvenile court have outstripped the system's ability to deal effectively with the crush of cases. The number of juvenile arrests has increased substantially over the past thirty years (Whitehead and Lab 1999, 14), and the number of juvenile court cases has also increased dramatically. In 1960, for example, there were an estimated 510,000 delinquency cases; by the end of the 1990s, there were almost 1 million delinquency cases handled each year by the various juvenile courts across the United States (Whitehead and Lab 1999, 15). These increases have burdened a system that has historically been inadequately funded. Courts are often understaffed, probation departments have too many cases for too few workers, and educational, recreational, and other prevention programs are woefully underfunded. When these two problems—the so-called nonsystem or inefficient nature of juvenile justice and the huge increase in cases—are combined, it is easy to see that the contemporary juvenile justice system is under severe strain.

Another difficult and controversial issue facing juvenile justice today is deciding what to do with serious juvenile offenders. In response to the public's perception that the juvenile justice system slaps youthful offenders on the wrist, many states have passed laws that make it easier to try juveniles as adults. This process is known as transfer or waiver. A waiver may occur in several different ways. One such method is known as statutory exclusion or legislative waiver (Whitehead and Lab 1999, 221). The way this form of waiver works is fairly straightforward: state legislatures simply pass laws requiring that certain offenses (such as murder) be automatically handled by the adult criminal justice system, regardless of the age of the suspected offender. Of course, this kind of legislation may get lawmakers and prosecutors into trouble if the suspect is very young, particularly since anyone under the age of seven in U.S. court jurisdictions cannot be tried for a crime.

An alternative type of waiver involves prosecutorial discretion. That is, the prosecutor's office is empowered and authorized to try a case in juvenile or adult court, depending on which the prosecutor believes to be most appropriate. Finally, in many juvenile court systems the prosecution may request a waiver hearing. At such a hearing, the juvenile judge must decide if the youth in question should remain in the juvenile system or be transferred to the adult criminal justice system.

An increasing number of juveniles are being transferred to the adult criminal justice system—a trend that has been apparent for some time now. Today there are approximately 10,000 juveniles waived to the adult court each year (Snyder et al. 2001), although waivers still represent a very small proportion of all juvenile delinquency cases, less than 5 percent nationally. Nonetheless, while it is clear that the number of transfers is larger than the rates of the 1970s and 1980s, it is not clear whether transfers are an effective response to serious delinquency. While some studies find that transferred youth are more likely to be incarcerated and for longer periods of time than youth who remain in the juvenile system (thus satisfying the public's desire for harsher treatment), other studies find that transferred youth are actually treated more leniently in the adult system than they would have been had they stayed in the juvenile system (Whitehead and Lab 1999, 223). The reason for this leniency is that some judges in the adult system treat the transferred juvenile as a first-time offender (that is, it is the juvenile's first offense as an adult), and such offenders typically receive lighter sentences than repeat offenders. In addition, although juveniles who end up in the adult court system are charged with serious crimes, they may not always be intimidating in appearance or demeanor. Sometimes youngsters appearing in an adult courtroom setting may appear disarmingly innocent to judges and juries, and thus in need of protection and supervision rather than punishment.

An important question to raise is whether transferred youth are more or less likely to reoffend, compared to youth who remain in the juvenile system. Although there is limited evidence, in general, it does not appear that transfer leads to lower rates of recidivism. As Whitehead and Lab (1999, 223) report, "Recidivism statistics do not indicate any advantage for transferred youth." Indeed, some studies find that transferred youth are more likely to reoffend (Bishop et al. 1996; Winner et al. 1996). The reasons for this increased rate of reoffending among those youth transferred to the adult criminal justice system are unclear. One possible explanation is that transferred youth are exposed to the harsh conditions of prison life, not to mention the potential for abuse of young people in adult prisons. While many states try to separate juveniles from adults in the correctional system, such separation is neither automatic nor continuous, and opportunities for adult influences and abusive behavior toward juveniles is always a possibility. The limited and less than impressive findings regarding the effectiveness of transfer notwithstanding, Whitehead and Lab (1999, 223) conclude, "Nevertheless, the current climate favoring punishment suggests that transfer and other mechanisms to get juveniles into adult court will continue."

Another controversial issue facing the juvenile justice system is divestiture, which refers to the removal of status offenders from the juvenile court's jurisdiction. Proponents of divestiture argue that the juvenile court should focus its attention and limited resources on the more serious problems of delinquency, particularly violent delinquency. In addition, there is a concern that processing status offenders through the juvenile justice system may actually backfire, leading to more rather than less misbehavior. This concern is based on the notion that status offenders may learn to become more delinquent as a result of being exposed to more serious offenders. To date, several states (e.g., Maine and Washington) have already instituted a policy of divestiture; other states have retained jurisdiction over status offenders but have instituted a policy of deinstitutionalization for status offenders (Whitehead and Lab 1999, 388). Deinstitutionalization simply refers to the policy of handling status offenders in the community rather than placing them in juvenile institutions.

Female offenders would be particularly affected by a policy of deinstitutionalization for status offenses (Acoca 2004). Girls are much more likely than boys to become involved in the juvenile justice system because of status offense charges. Approximately 24 percent of girls and 4 percent of boys housed in detention center have been placed there for status offenses. Girls who commit status offenses typically run away from home, mostly to escape physical, emotional, or sexual abuse. After their arrest, these female status offenders are placed in juvenile detention centers with little or no specialized treatment for their previous experiences of abuse. If the juvenile justice system were no longer to consider status offenses to be criminal, the number of girls housed in detention centers would dramatically decrease. However, female status offenders are placed in detention centers because there is nowhere else to place them. Therefore, deinstitutionalization would require the development of gender-specific treatment programs (Acoca 2004).

Divestiture is not without its share of critics, however. The opponents of divestiture argue that today's status offender may become tomorrow's delinquent. Without the intervention of the juvenile justice system, they argue, status offenders may travel down a path that leads to more serious problems. It is unclear at this time if the U.S. juvenile justice system will implement divestiture more widely. Although deinstitutionalization has generally been viewed as a major success, many juvenile judges and other juvenile justice professionals would prefer to keep jurisdiction over status offenders (Siegel and Senna 2000, 521). Thus, the controversy surrounding status offenders and divestiture has not been settled.

In addition to the questions of system disarray and overload, waiver, and divestiture, many observers of juvenile justice have argued that in the United States the system is biased against minorities and low-income youth and families. One of the most vocal critics of juvenile justice is Jerome Miller. In his book *Search and Destroy: African-American Males in the Criminal Justice System* (1996), Miller argues that the criminal justice system in general and the juvenile justice system in particular have devastated black families and communities across the country. Referring to the work of delinquency researchers Katherine Hunt Federle and Meda Chesney-Lind, Miller (1996, 78) agrees with their assessment that "the growth of the institutionalized minority population in the juvenile justice system can be explained only in terms of pervasive, systemic racism."

Many other researchers and observers of juvenile justice have been less critical than Miller, but they agree that minority youth are indeed more likely to be processed through the juvenile justice system as compared to their white counterparts. Further, it has been well documented that low-income youth are significantly more likely to be formally handled by the juvenile justice system than are juveniles from higher-income families (Snyder and Sickmund 1999). While it is not possible for us to conclude one way or the other that the juvenile justice system intentionally discriminates against minorities and poor youth, we can unequivocally say that minority and poor youth are overrepresented in the system. Understanding why this is so is a crucially important question. The two most logical possibilities would seem to be (1) minority and poor youth actually commit more delinquency or (2) the juvenile justice system is biased. (A third logical possibility simply combines these two possibilities.)

In either case, the fact that youth from these groups are overrepresented is cause enough for concern. Researchers must continue to study this problem so that solutions may be found.

Another problem is perhaps the most profound of all: we refer to it as the problem of identity crisis. One of the founding principles of the U.S. juvenile justice system is *parens patriae* (the state as parent) and the notion that the system should do what is in the best interests of the child. Today this guiding principle is being questioned. Indeed, in the past several decades, juvenile justice has increasingly come to resemble the adult criminal justice system (Berger 1996). Waiver, as discussed above, has been described as a possible step along a pathway that may lead to the elimination of the juvenile justice system (Whitehead and Lab 1999). We think this is an unlikely outcome, as juvenile justice has become embedded in the United States. Another challenge to the juvenile justice system is the large number of court cases, which has had an impact on the nature of juvenile courts as well as the rights of juveniles whose cases are heard in such court settings.

Legal Challenges to the Juvenile Justice System

The first delinquency law in 1899 was the culmination of a lot of hard work and effort on the part of many people over several decades. Along the way, the child savers encountered strong resistance to their goals and programs, resistance that did not disappear simply because new legislation was being passed. Some might say that the juvenile courts and the entire juvenile justice system created by this new legislation was only an experiment. Even if this is true or is the dominant position among lawmakers and those working with juvenile offenders, the system in place today is well established. While changes in the way juvenile offenders are processed may happen, and some have already occurred, a separate system of justice for juveniles will be here for a long time to come.

For the first few decades of the twentieth century, the fledgling juvenile justice system in the United States enjoyed a honeymoon period. By that, we mean that people seemed willing to give this new system a chance. Certainly, there were doubters and probably detractors of this new way of handling juvenile offenders, but serious challenges and threats to the constitutionality of the system were uncommon. One of the earliest challenges to the new system was a case decided in 1905, *Commonwealth v. Fisher*, decided by the Pennsylvania Supreme Court. Essentially, this decision allowed the state to imprison juveniles in state institutions until they were twenty-one years old, as provided in Pennsylvania's new delinquency law at that time. A similar decision was reached in Idaho a few years later.

These early twentieth-century court rulings gave added emphasis to the emerging juvenile court and delinquency law movements. Although most state governments and organizations favored the delinquency laws and the new system of justice created by these laws, there were some signs of disagreement and even suspicion regarding juvenile courts and the new laws. For example, a few decades after the U.S. Children's Bureau was established in 1912, the agency had issued studies and reports examining juvenile facilities in various states. Others began to write and voice concerns about the rights of juveniles in the system and their treatment at the hands of juvenile authorities.

For the most part, however, juvenile delinquency laws and the newly developing juvenile justice system were virtually unchallenged in the courts during the first half of the twentieth century. Many people may have been encouraged by the low rates of delinquency that occurred during the Great Depression of the 1930s. Perhaps, too, people were willing to allow this new experiment time to develop.

This attitude began to change, and significantly so, in the 1960s. In that decade, and for years to come, appellate courts began to accept cases claiming abuse of juveniles' rights and instances of abuse within the juvenile justice system. These court cases began to change the way in which courts and institutions were operated, from a "kindly parent" model to a much more legalistic and formal system, patterned in many ways after the criminal justice system for adults.

The first case in which the U.S. Supreme Court granted juveniles a right to a lawyer was *Kent v. United States*, which was decided in 1966. Morris Kent was a sixteen-year-old living in Washington, D.C., who was arrested for housebreaking, forcible rape, and robbery. He was taken to a detention house and stayed there for about one week before he admitted to the charges and was sent to a juvenile home. Later, a juvenile court judge ruled that his case should be transferred to the adult federal court system in

Washington. Kent's mother hired a lawyer to fight for his rights, but the juvenile court judge decided to transfer the case anyway, despite holding no hearings and receiving no recommendations that this was the best course of action in the case. Kent's attorney even asked for a hearing to determine his client's sanity, but that motion was also denied. Eventually, Kent was convicted in adult court of two of the charges against him. He was ultimately ruled not guilty by reason of insanity on the rape charge. Why he was convicted on two counts but ruled insane for a third charge, all of which were part of one criminal event, is not clear. The attorney for Kent appealed the convictions, and the case was carried all the way to the U.S. Supreme Court. In 1966, the Court ruled in favor of Kent and overturned his convictions on the grounds that he was not given counsel prior to his confession and that the juvenile court judge never provided any written reasons why the case was being transferred to the adult system. In addition, the Court ruled that the doctrine of *parens patriae* did not give states the right to trample on the legal rights of youth.

Although the *Kent* case was the first one to grant the right of counsel for juvenile defendants who are facing criminal charges, it also concerned federal jurisdictions and the issue of waiver or transfer. However, another Supreme Court case—*In re Gault,* which was decided in 1967—had a more far-reaching effect on the rights of juveniles in the courts, and even in the streets. In this case, Gerald Gault, a fifteen-year-old Arizona boy, and his friend were accused by a neighbor of making an obscene phone call. The police arrested the boy at his home, without his parents' knowledge. Already on probation for another crime, Gault was given two hearings, without legal representation, and with the accuser not present. Gault was ultimately convicted of the charge against him and sentenced to the Arizona Industrial School for an unspecified period of time, or until he reached the age of twenty-one; that is, up to six years. Interestingly, had Gault been an adult, the maximum time he would have served for the crime was two months.

Upon examination of the case, the U.S. Supreme Court overturned Gault's conviction on several grounds, grounds that have now become standard protections in the operation of U.S. juvenile courts. Among the legal rights granted to Gault, and by extension to all future juvenile criminal defendants, were the right to an attorney (in cases involving potential confinement in an institution), the right to cross-examine witnesses giving evidence against you, and the right to remain silent (the Fifth Amendment right). In essence, the Supreme Court ruled in this case that juveniles have the same rights that adults do, although perhaps not to the same degree that adults do. What had been developed for over 100 years—namely, the almost reckless disregard for the rights of juveniles in an effort to serve their "best interests"—had been overturned, or at least subjected to careful scrutiny by the courts.

After the *Gault* case, there were several other Supreme Court cases, that added more rights to juveniles processed in juvenile courts throughout the nation. The courts stopped short, however, of making the juvenile court a miniature adult court. That is to say, the U.S. Supreme Court has given juveniles many of the same rights that adults enjoy, but not every right that adults have. For example, in the case *McKeiver v. Pennsylvania*, the court ruled that jury trials are not mandated in juvenile court. In this case, sixteen-year-old Joseph McKeiver was charged with several serious crimes, including robbery and receiving stolen property. His case was heard in juvenile court, where he was found delinquent of the charges against him. Although McKeiver had requested a jury trial in juvenile court, the judge ruled against his request. After his conviction in juvenile court, McKeiver appealed the verdict. The case went all the way to the U.S. Supreme Court, along with similar cases from Pennsylvania and North Carolina. In all three cases, the Court ruled against the defendants, arguing, in essence, that jury trials are not required for defendants in juvenile court. Among the stated reasons for reaching this decision, the Court argued that jury trials are not necessary for the fact-finding functions of juvenile courts and would not serve the purpose of providing proper treatment and rehabilitative services for youth. The Court did rule, however, that jury trials might be used in juvenile court cases as an option. Currently, about ten states use jury trials for juveniles, but in all of these states, jury trials are supervised by juvenile court judges and are reserved for less serious cases, such as status offenses.

In 1984, the U.S. Supreme Court heard *New Jersey v. T.L.O.* This case focused on the issue of searches of students on school grounds. In particular, the case involved two female students who were charged with smoking cigarettes in a restroom in a New Jersey high school. When one of the girls, T.L.O., protested her innocence, the assistant principal of the school demanded to look into her purse, supposedly for evidence of cigarettes. When he examined her purse, the administrator found evidence of

marijuana possession, including a pipe and written material indicating the intent of T.L.O. to sell marijuana. She later confessed
to the police that she in fact had been using and selling marijuana. T.L.O. was subsequently found delinquent of the charges
against her in juvenile court, but she appealed her conviction on
the grounds that the evidence used against her was seized un-
constitutionally. The Supreme Court of New Jersey upheld
T.L.O.'s appeal, on the grounds that the evidence was in fact un-
constitutionally gathered. Ultimately, the U.S. Supreme Court accepted the case and heard evidence from both sides. The Court
ruled that T.L.O.'s original conviction should be upheld, on the
grounds that a school has the right to protect its property and the
safety of its students from criminal behavior, and this protection
can take the form of searches of student possessions. The Court
was sensitive to the rights of students, however, and acknowledged that not just any search of lockers, purses, and other possessions of students are permissible. Rather, the Court emphasized that student possessions can be searched by school officials
or law enforcement officers if the search is connected with a "reasonable" belief that there is evidence of criminal activity in the
student's possession(s).

The "reasonable evidence" issue resurfaced in a case decided
in June 2002, *Board of Education of Independent School District No. 92
of Pottawatomie County et al. v. Earls et al.* At issue in this case was a
school policy in Tecumseh, Oklahoma, that allowed school administrators and teachers to search the property of students who
were participating in any extracurricular activities, including student athletes, in order to prevent drug possession and drug
abuse. In the original case, teachers and school administrators reported that they had seen students using drugs at school and on
school property. In response, the school board passed a policy
that required all middle and high school students to submit to
urinalysis tests, even if there was no suspicion of drug use for a
particular student, if they wanted to participate in extracurricular
events. Some parents challenged this policy because they thought
it violated the rights of students under the protection of the
Fourth Amendment to the U.S. Constitution, which protects citizens against unreasonable search and seizure. The case was first
heard in a U.S. district court, which ruled in favor of the school
district. The court argued that the drug-testing policy was fair
and reasonable and did not violate the constitutional rights of students. The case was then appealed to the Tenth Circuit, and the

original decision was overturned, the court ruling in favor of the students and their parents. Finally, the case was appealed to the U.S. Supreme Court, which ruled again in favor of the school district, and there the issue was settled. In its justifications for reaching their decision, the Supreme Court judges argued that drug testing, even for non-extracurricular participation, was justified in order for school systems to protect themselves against the effects of drug use among students. The health of students and all those connected with schools is too important to be negated by rigid testing policies. Therefore, it was reasoned, even "suspicionless" drug testing is allowable, given the school system's desire and need to detect and prevent drug use and abuse. Thus, the need for protection and immediate action to deter drug use in a school system offset the rights of students in this case.

As the debate among different courts in this case indicates, the protection of students' rights versus those of schools and the state to protect property and people is a sensitive issue. The state and U.S. Supreme courts have ruled that students are subject to searches and similar restraints of liberty given reasonable evidence that they have committed a crime. Many school districts have gone beyond the limits set by the courts in ordering searches of lockers, cars, purses, and other possessions of students while they are at school or on school grounds. Often, the judges' rulings seemed to have favored a school system's safety over students' rights, particularly when drug use is concerned. However, as Siegel and Senna (2000, 485) put it, in matters such as searches of student property and possessions, "School administrators are walking a tightrope between the students' constitutional rights to privacy and school safety."

There is little doubt that juvenile justice has undergone tremendous change over the years. The founders of the juvenile court would likely be surprised to see today's system, with its emphasis on legal formality and punishment. Now that we have identified and discussed some of the most pressing problems facing juvenile justice, we shift our focus to possible solutions.

Possible Solutions

While it is certainly the case that the juvenile justice system faces many problems, and while it is also true that rehabilitative efforts have something of a poor track record (Martinson 1974), it should not be concluded that nothing works when it comes to dealing with juvenile delinquents. In fact, we now know that there are programs and policies that are able to reduce, although not entirely eliminate, serious and violent delinquency and crime (University of Maryland 1997; Lundman 2001). There are also many programs and policies that, although popular with politicians and the public (e.g., boot camps), do not reduce serious delinquency and crime (Lundman 2001; Walker 2001). We will examine some of the most promising programs and policies.

In the most comprehensive review of the existing crime and delinquency literature to date, a team of researchers from the University of Maryland (1997), headed by noted criminologist Lawrence Sherman, wrote a report to the U.S. Congress, *Preventing Crime: What Works, What Doesn't, What's Promising*, summarizing the current state of knowledge about crime and delinquency intervention and prevention programs. Anyone with an interest in juvenile and criminal justice would be wise to study this report carefully (available online at http://www.ncjrs.org/works/). The report reaches a number of conclusions, not all of which can be reviewed here. The most important conclusions for our purposes are easy to summarize. Sherman and his colleagues reach the following conclusions:

- Many solutions to crime and delinquency are best found outside the criminal justice system.
- Unfortunately, crime and delinquency prevention programs seem to work best in communities that need them the least.
- High-crime communities that are most in need of innovative programs and policies are also the most difficult to reach.
- The underlying causes of crime and delinquency are to be found in social structural conditions, such as social inequality and concentrated poverty.

Sherman and his colleagues state their primary conclusion clearly and succinctly:

This report found that some prevention programs work, some do not, some are promising, and some have not been tested adequately. Given the evidence of promising and effective programs, the Report finds that the effectiveness of Department of Justice funding depends heavily on whether it is directed to the urban neighborhoods where youth violence is highly concentrated. Substantial reductions in national rates of serious crime can only be achieved by prevention in areas of concentrated poverty, where the majority of all homicides in the nation occur, and where homicide rates are 20 times the national average. (University of Maryland, 1977).

The report is important for several reasons. For one, it is the most up-to-date and most comprehensive review of the crime and delinquency prevention literature currently available. For another, it correctly points out the need to address multiple problems and social contexts, particularly in the most crime-ridden neighborhoods. And finally, it shows convincingly that the "nothing works" argument is false.

Currently, there are several specific policies and programs that appear to be promising as possible solutions to the problem of crime and delinquency. Although the available evaluation data are limited at this time, there is much hope and excitement surrounding what has come to be known as restorative justice. Originally developed overseas, in countries such as New Zealand and Australia, restorative justice emphasizes the need for a balanced approach to delinquency. One of the most popular restorative justice programs brings together victims, offenders, and their social supports (friends and family) in a head-to-head meeting, or conference, among the offender, the victim, members of the community, and other interested parties. At such group conferences, the victims of delinquency are able to express their hurt, anger, and fear. This is thought to lead to healing and closure for some victims. Also, such conferences are expected to allow offenders to learn that their actions have been harmful to a real, flesh-and-blood human being, not some faceless, nameless entity. While this approach is most appropriate for nonviolent offenses, it appears to be a promising alternative to current juvenile justice practices (Whitehead and Lab 1999, 372). Conceptually, this approach combines restorative justice with reintegrative shaming, which means that the offender is shamed into reconciliation with the victim and members of the community in a process of being reintegrated into the community (Braithwaite 1989).

According to some (McCold 1999), all restorative justice practices must at least involve face-to-face interactions between victim and offender, and such meetings influence what happens to both the victim and the offender, presumably especially to the offender. Gordon Bazemore (2001) and colleagues (Bazemore and Umbreit 2001) describe several examples of restorative justice models operating in the United States. Many are based on the idea of victim-offender mediations and family-group conferences. Another example of restorative justice models is peacemaking or sentencing circles, which are found in Canada, Minnesota, and Colorado. This model attempts to bring resolutions to arguments and claims against members of the community, claims such as juvenile offenses. Peacemaking circles are thought to stem from Native American traditions, so their existence is long standing. Then there are reparative boards, which are found in Vermont, Arizona, California, and Colorado, and merchant accountability boards, which include members of the larger community and work to help offenders see the costs and effects of their crimes, including the effects on small businesses in a community.

Although reintegrative shaming and restorative justice may work well, especially in those societies that are organized according to communal values (Braithwaite 1989), the concept may not be as easily applied in all societies. In the Philippines, for example, there is a long-standing sociolegal arrangement for handling neighborhood disputes, including many juvenile offenses, in a *barangay* court. This system does not allow lawyers to be present in the court proceedings and is based on the conciliatory powers of an elected official, a *barangay* captain, to resolve disputes and arguments, as well as minor criminal charges, amicably and fairly to the satisfaction of most, if not all, disputants. Although the Philippines can be characterized as a "communal" society, in that social relationships are often focused around the family and neighborhood, the country does not have a large, bureaucratic welfare system. In addition, Philippine society stresses the avoidance of shame, or *hiya*, as much as possible, especially when shame is reflected on the family or *barkada*, which is a close, peer group (Lynch 1970; Lynch and de Guzman 1973). Therefore, a practice of mediation and reconciliation, accompanied by attempts to reintegrate an offender into the community, would make sense in a society with similar values and social structure.

In the United States, however, the emphasis on individualism and individual responsibility for behavior would seem to work against an effective implementation of restorative justice. Despite this possible disclaimer, research is beginning to demonstrate that restorative justice works not only in other countries but in the United States as well, at least to some degree (Bazemore 2001; Hay 2001).

In 1993, the Office of Juvenile Justice and Delinquency Prevention (OJJDP) set aside grant money for the Balanced and Restorative Justice Project (Office of Juvenile Justice and Delinquency Prevention 1998). The goal of this project was to provide technical assistance and training for restorative justice programs nationwide. In order to achieve this goal, the OJJDP funded programs in Palm Beach County, Florida; Allegheny County, Pennsylvania; and Dakota County, Minnesota. The mistakes and successes of these programs would allow for the development of better programs in the future. Each of the programs is based on the idea of restorative justice and promotes accountability, competency development, and community safety. The project utilizes programs such as restitution, community service, and victim-offender mediation. There are now Balanced and Restorative Justice programs in all fifty states. Because the majority of these programs are either in the development or early implementation phases, there is not any research available regarding the programs' success (Office of Juvenile Justice and Delinquency Prevention 1998).

One restorative justice program that has been shown to be effective is the teen court. Teen courts began in Texas in the late 1980s as an alternative to juvenile court for first-time misdemeanor offenders (Zehner 1997). In this program, a teen who is charged with a misdemeanor goes before a court where peers fill all the roles within the court. Therefore, the lawyers, judge, and jurors also are teens under adult supervision. In order to participate in the court, the defendant must plead guilty to the charge. Next, the defense attorney submits mitigating factors for jurors to consider, such as school grades, behavior, and extracurricular activities. The jury then decides upon a sentence for the defendant. The sentences generally range from community service to restitution for victims. The defendant then has thirty days to adhere to the sentence or he or she will be sent to regular juvenile court (Zehner 1997).

According to evaluation research, teen court is a promising restorative justice program. In Alaska and Missouri, juveniles referred to teen court were significantly less likely to recidivate six months following their original offense (Butts, Buck, and Coggeshall 2002). In Florida, those who participated in teen courts improved their self-esteem and had more respect for authority, while only 12.6 percent reoffended within five months of their original charge (Harrison, Maupin, and Mays 2001). Those who participated in teen courts in Kentucky between 1994 and 1998 also did well: 70 percent of referrals completed the program and less than one-third recidivated within one year of the original referral (Minor, Wells, and Soderstrom 1999). Teen courts also are cheaper to run and cost less than $300 per referral, in comparison to $3,000 for a child to go to juvenile court and receive probation (Zehner 1997).

Community policing efforts are sometimes considered to be part of a restorative justice approach. Community policing is more of a philosophy than a specific set of policies or practices. The idea is to get the police and members of the community working together to prevent and control crime and delinquency. A special emphasis is placed on preventing delinquency rather than reacting to it after the fact. Police officers work to be seen by citizens as helpful partners in the fight against crime. There is mounting evidence that community-oriented policing is an effective way to reduce crime and delinquency. It is a bright spot in recent juvenile and adult criminal justice policy.

In addition to family conferences and other types of victim-offender reconciliation programs and community-oriented policing efforts, restorative justice is attractive as a philosophy. Since it emphasizes accountability (which should please "get tough" conservatives), skills and competency development for offenders (which should please treatment-oriented liberals), and protection of the community (which should please everyone), this approach should have widespread appeal. Some of the leading figures and researchers in restorative justice (e.g., Bazemore and Umbreit 1994) have begun to offer evidence of the effectiveness of restorative justice programs and policies. However, as Walker (2001) points out, we do not yet fully know how effective such programs and policies are. What is needed at this time is more careful and comprehensive evaluations (University of Maryland 1997).

Another promising approach to the treatment and prevention of delinquency can be found in improved counseling techniques and treatment programs that have been developed over the past twenty years. In particular, researchers and authors such as James Garbarino (1999), Richard Lundman (2001), and Larry Siegel and Joseph Senna (2000) have all concluded that much of the individualized treatment programs of the past are simply failures. However, newer forms of treatment—for example, Scott Henggeler's multisystemic therapy (MST)—do appear to be successful at reducing recidivism. MST focuses on multiple issues (or "systems"; hence the name), including (1) family dynamics (parent-child, sibling-sibling, etc.) and communication; (2) thinking patterns and behavioral problems of the troubled youth; (3) decision-making and interpersonal skills; (4) peer relationships; and (5) parenting training (Garbarino 1999, 209). This more comprehensive type of treatment has shown promising initial results. Henggeler and his colleagues have been able to substantially lower recidivism rates, even for chronic juvenile offenders. One evaluation of MST found that four years after treatment, only 22 percent of MST youth were recidivists, compared to 72 percent of youth who went through traditional individual counseling (Siegel and Senna 2000, 621). While MST and other similar treatment programs look promising, more evaluation of such programs is needed. If evidence continues to mount in favor of these programs, they should be expanded to reach more youth and families.

An additional approach to delinquency prevention and treatment is often given generic labels, such as "alternatives to incarceration" or "alternative sentencing." One of the main proponents of this approach is Jerome Miller, former commissioner of the Department of Youth Services in Massachusetts. Miller became famous when he ordered the closing of all juvenile institutions in his state. Only a handful of juvenile offenders were held in secure placement, and the vast majority of juvenile offenders were released back into the community. Miller correctly recognized that most of the youth in the state's training schools were not hardened, violent offenders. Indeed, most were property offenders and amenable to treatment in the community (as opposed to incarceration in a juvenile correctional facility). According to his own account of this reform effort, Miller suggests that changes in the system were often met with resistance and even sabotage, particularly by staff members and administrators within the state's juvenile correctional system. For example, Miller saw an escape map pinned to the door of an institutional supervisor's office, with a sign indicating the free distribution of the map. The supervisor thought it was a joke, but that particular institution experienced a large increase in escape attempts during the time Miller was trying to implement changes in the state's juvenile correctional system (Miller 1991, chap. 8). Although Miller's Massachusetts experiment, as it has been called, was initially controversial, today it can be viewed as a successful example of how to improve the juvenile justice system (Miller 1991; Ohlin, Miller, and Coates n.d.; Lundman 2001, 225–234). Nearly thirty years after the closing of the juvenile institutions in Massachusetts, the state still has a low rate of commitment to public juvenile institutions, but a large rate of commitment and referral to private ones (Lundman 2001, 232).

Few states have gone so far as Massachusetts, however, in addressing problems at juvenile institutions. Accounts of Miller's efforts have detailed the numerous incidents of organized resistance to his plan, efforts often initiated or encouraged by the staff members at these juvenile institutions. A replication of the Massachusetts experiment was tried in Maryland in 1988 and was evaluated as unsuccessful. Even in this case, however, the evaluators concluded that the juvenile arrest rates for violent crimes and other serious crimes in Maryland, and self-admitted rates of delinquency among samples of youth surveyed before and after the experiment, were not higher after the deinstitutionalization experiment, an indication that the reform effort did not reduce public safety (Lundman 2001, 233).

Despite the reluctance of states to follow Miller's example in Massachusetts, and despite the resistance that can be expected when such reform efforts are presented for public support, the Massachusetts experiment remains a bold effort in the history of our country's attempts to control delinquency with cost-effective yet relatively safe measures. Today, Miller heads up the National Center on Institutions and Alternatives (NCIA). He continues to be a major advocate for young people. His commitment to the well-being of juveniles and the reform of juvenile justice is commendable.

Many other juvenile justice advocates and researchers are calling for more deinstitutionalization and other alternatives to incarceration (such as drug courts). There is a growing awareness that only a few juveniles (proportionally speaking) pose a serious threat to others. These few but very violent juveniles should certainly be placed in secure programs where they cannot violate and victimize people. Most juvenile offenders are not violent, and they can be successfully treated and monitored in the community.

Drug courts represent a new approach to society's reaction to drug offenders. The first drug court was established in Dade County, Florida, in 1989 in response to the rising number of prisoners sentenced to lengthy terms of incarceration for drug offenses. In 1993, the first juvenile drug court was established in Key West, Florida. Today, there are over 500 adult drug courts and 160 juvenile or family drug courts in the United States (Belenko 2001). Many similar alternative courts are spreading throughout the country, such as mental health courts and community courts; some prefer the rubric of "problem-solving courts" to cover all of these manifestations of the drug court concept (Freeman-Wilson, Sullivan, and Weinstein 2003). However, for the remainder of this discussion, the general term *drug court* will be used.

While drug courts may be varied in their approach to handling drug offenders, there are certain national guidelines that have been established for all drug courts—adult and juvenile—to meet (Drug Court Standards Committee 1997). For example, drug courts are often referred to as drug treatment courts, which tends to stamp them as treatment oriented, at least as much as they are punitive. In addition, drug court participants are required to plead guilty to a drug offense and to voluntarily submit to the drug court program for at least one year before being admitted into the program. In the past, only nonviolent offenders and drug users, as opposed to drug dealers, were permitted into drug court programs, but these restrictions are gradually being lifted as more drug courts are being created and as evaluations of existing ones are being published. Once a participant has been admitted to the program, the presence of lawyers is lessened. All participants are required to appear before a higher court judge on a regular basis, first weekly, then, over time, on a monthly basis. Lawyers do not usually represent participants at these court appearances unless a participant is suspected of committing new crimes while in the program. In addition, participants are required to attend regular treatment sessions and to submit to weekly urine screens, to ensure they are staying off of drugs. Adults are expected to obtain and keep employment, and juveniles are expected to finish school if they have not graduated by the time they enter the program.

Drug courts offer a balance of treatment and punishment to effect significant changes in the lives of participants. The drug court team is represented by members of the criminal justice system and treatment professionals, and school personnel for juveniles. All of the team members meet weekly to discuss the progress of each participant. Knowledge is regularly and openly shared among all team members, which often results in an effective response to an individual's drug problems. Judges have considerable latitude to impose sanctions on those who are not complying with the rules of the drug court. Sanctions are typically graduated in terms of severity and often range from increased urine screens, to increased court appearances, to increased school-related activities (for juveniles), to jail or detention time, and ultimately, to dismissal from the program.

Evaluations of drug court programs usually conclude that they are more effective than traditional methods of handling drug offenders, especially incarceration or imprisonment for drug users, although not all evaluations are as positive (Robinson 2000; Belenko 2001). Drug court graduates usually commit crimes, including drug-related offenses, at a lower rate than do nongraduates, again with some exceptions. In addition, drug courts usually cost far less to operate than traditional prisons or detention centers, but they are not as cost-effective as regular probation. On a more negative side, however, the graduation rates of drug courts are around 50 percent—although some courts graduate at rates of over 60 percent—and graduation rates for juvenile drug courts are often lower, with rates well under 50 percent (Belenko 2001). Overall, drug courts represent a good alternative to traditional, more punitive methods of handling drug offenders, youth and adult alike. Despite some negative results of drug court evaluations, the continued existence and development of these kinds of alternative methods of handling young and adult offenders with drug problems seems reasonably assured.

Another alternative to traditional incarceration involves correctional boot camp programs. Correctional boot camps were first implemented for adults in 1983 and were viewed as an alternative to incarceration that fit well with "get tough on crime" policies (Armstrong, Gover, and MacKenzie 2002). By 1995, there were thirty-seven correctional juvenile boot camps in operation. Correctional boot camps are similar to military-style boot camps: in both types of camps, physical exercise, discipline, and respect for authority are emphasized; however, correctional boot camps also incorporate treatment and education. Correctional boot camps vary from program to program in their emphasis on discipline and treatment. Some boot camps, for example, focus more heavily on the military and discipline aspects of the program, while others focus more on counseling, drug treatment, and education. The percentage of treatment versus discipline depends upon the program (Armstrong, Gover, and MacKenzie 2002). The typical juvenile offender in a correctional boot camp is a young male between the ages of fourteen and eighteen who has been convicted of a nonviolent offense (MacKenzie and Rosay 1996). Juvenile offenders are generally sent to correctional boot camps by a juvenile court judge, whereas adults who are eligible for correctional boot camps are allowed to decide between boot camps and other sanctions (Armstrong, Gover, and MacKenzie 2002).

Correctional boot camps were originally developed to help with prison overcrowding. It was believed that because participants' stay at the boot camp would be shorter, such programs would be a cheaper alternative. However, many juveniles who would have been placed on probation were instead being placed in boot camps, causing a net-widening effect. Therefore, more people were being incarcerated because juveniles who previously would not have been incarcerated were being sent to correctional boot camps (Armstrong, Gover, and MacKenzie 2002).

Overall, correctional boot camps have been found to be ineffective in reducing recidivism rates for juvenile offenders. Evaluations for both juvenile and adult correctional boot camp programs show no reduction in recidivism, and those who participated in the programs have similar recidivism rates as those who experienced traditional incarceration (Zhang 2000; Armstrong, Gover, and MacKenzie 2002; California Department of Youth Authority 1997). In some cases, recidivism for correctional boot camp participants was higher than those placed in traditional detention centers. These juveniles had higher recidivism rates because their probation officers watch them more closely after their release from camp than they did other juvenile probationers. This led to boot camp probationers receiving more technical violations than other juvenile probationers (California Department of Youth Authority 1997).

Although research shows that correctional boot camps are not effective in reducing recidivism for adults or juveniles, they remain a popular alternative. The public wants offenders to be punished and to pay for their crimes, and boot camps provide an alternative to the prison system, which is often viewed as a place to warehouse instead of rehabilitate or punish offenders. However, offenders, whether imprisoned or placed in correctional boot camps, will return to the communities from which they came. Unfortunately, many of these communities are experiencing social disorganization and poverty, providing the environment for one to easily recidivate upon return.

Another alternative to traditional incarceration is the use of therapeutic communities within the detention center itself. Therapeutic communities can be used to address a variety of treatment issues, including substance abuse, prior abuse or neglect, and the lack of positive social interaction or coping skills. Therapeutic communities are based on a self-help model, where participants are encouraged to examine their problems in a holistic manner. If a therapeutic community focused on substance abuse, for example, participants would be encouraged to focus not only on their addiction but also on the underlying issues of why they are abusing substances. The offenders would also be simultaneously developing positive coping skills and learning how to interact with others in a community setting (Lockwood, McCorkel, and Inciardi 1998).

Therapeutic communities are separated from the rest of the general population in order to foster a positive social environment. This model allows the individual to develop coping skills, such as problem solving and how to seek social support from others. The new coping skills allow participants to handle everyday situations that provoke stress while reinforcing the idea of living within a community.

Therapeutic communities have enjoyed successful results in adult prisons around the country and have been "accepted as the most effective kind of prison drug abuse treatment intervention" (Wexler 1995, 58). For example, Martin et al. (1996) evaluated a therapeutic community in a California prison after its three-year period of existence. More than 40 percent of the general population in the prison lacked a high school diploma or GED, and the majority of inmates admitted to engaging in high-risk behavior for HIV. Martin et al. (1996), however, found only an 8 percent recidivism rate at twelve months for those inmates who completed the therapeutic community program and participated in twelve months of aftercare. The researchers also found only a 14 percent recidivism rate for those inmates who completed the therapeutic community program and twenty-four months of aftercare. Wexler, Falkin, and Lipton (1988) also evaluated the first three years of a therapeutic community program in the New York prison system called "Stay'n Out." The researchers found that those men and women who completed the program were less likely to have parole revocations than those participants who dropped out of the program before six months.

Therapeutic communities also have been shown to be effective with substance-abusing female inmates because "this approach invites clients and practitioners to explore the many issues and experiences that frame the client's substance use, thereby ensuring that gender-specific issues facing women clients will be addressed" (Lockwood, McCorkel, and Inciardi 1998, 195).

Currently, therapeutic communities are more likely to be found in an adult facility. However, this approach to treatment could also be used in a female juvenile detention center because female juvenile delinquents are more likely to have experienced prior physical/sexual abuse and prior physical/emotional neglect than male juvenile delinquents. Treatment programs developed for boys may not take into consideration girls' unique experiences. Therefore, allowing these young girls to explore their problems in a safe and secure environment (the separated community) while learning positive problem-solving and social interaction skills could help promote healing and reductions in recidivism as it has for adult female offenders.

Another approach to reducing delinquency and generally improving the lives of children is the boldest and perhaps the most controversial, but also potentially the most effective. Along with many other observers and critics of juvenile justice, we believe that an ounce of prevention is worth a pound of cure. That is, prevention and early intervention should be the primary focus of any society's policies and programs to reduce delinquency. Today, unfortunately, we react to the problems experienced and created by juveniles rather than trying to prevent them in the first place.

The Oregon Social Learning Center (OSLC) was created by Gerald Patterson and is based on the concept that effective parenting skills are one of the better delinquency prevention methods in U.S. society. It is one of several family-parenting programs available throughout the United States, including Functional

Family Therapy. The OSLC uses various methods to teach parents effective ways of parenting children, including difficult-to-handle adolescents. The center often deals with families of youth who are already involved in the juvenile justice system or are at high risk for such involvement. It emphasizes skillful handling of potentially disruptive and volatile situations with love, patience, and understanding rather than the use of harsh discipline, yelling, and physical punishment. Behavioral management tools are also taught and emphasized in the philosophy of the OSLC, including time-out for youth who are having a particularly difficult time controlling their behavior. Time-out means children are allowed to go to their rooms, or some other place where they can be alone, to think about their behavior and how they may have contributed to the conflict. Rules and duties for youth are stressed for good behavioral results, but only if they are consistently enforced with patience and understanding.

Evaluations of the OSLC and similar programs typically find that they are at least as effective as alternative methods of child-rearing, as far as crime prevention is concerned, and that they usually cost far less than placing youth into institutional settings (Siegel 2002; Siegel and Senna 2000).

The University of Maryland report, discussed earlier, reaches a number of important conclusions, one of which is the need to address underlying social structural conditions if we are to significantly reduce and prevent crime and delinquency. What does it mean to address and change social structural conditions? Among other things, it requires that we recognize that social patterns—such as chronic unemployment, poverty, and racism—are key causal influences on delinquency and crime. Finding ways to improve the conditions that give rise to delinquency and crime, as well as increasing the opportunities for the country's poorest communities, must become a priority.

One of the earliest crime and delinquency prevention programs was the Chicago Area Project (CAP). The original CAP was implemented in 1934; it was one of the first attempts to rehabilitate juvenile offenders in a community setting (Kobrin 1966). Based on research conducted by Clifford Shaw and Henry McKay (see Chapter 4), it was discovered that there were high rates of delinquency in certain areas of the city largely because of recent influxes of immigrants. These immigrants had originally come from rural areas and were now learning to live and survive in an urban setting. This proved to be difficult for many of the new immigrants who lacked resources and the skills necessary to survive in the city. Many of the immigrants' children became delinquent as they, too, attempted to learn to survive in a new environment that had few social resources or controls. Shaw and McKay concluded that these delinquent children were offending in order to fit into their new environments and to find status. Previously, delinquency had been viewed as an indication that something was wrong with the person; Shaw and McKay concluded that delinquent behavior was a rational response given the circumstances, such as living in high-delinquency neighborhoods, which were also characterized by other patterns of illness and urban decay. The researchers concluded that delinquency could be prevented or reversed and that it was an issue of environmental decay rather than a personal problem (Kobrin 1966).

Clifford R. Shaw developed the CAP in order to address the high rates of delinquency found in the inner city and to prevent future delinquency (Kobrin 1966). In order to accomplish this change in behavior patterns, Shaw first recognized that the community itself would have to become involved in the effort to reduce or prevent delinquency. This community involvement was necessary because "a delinquency program could hardly hope to be effective unless and until the aims of such a program became the aims of the local population" (Kobrin 1966, 476). Shaw also wanted to use already established religious, economic, and political networks in this new delinquency prevention program by guiding these groups to implement and run welfare programs of their own (Kobrin 1966).

In order to prevent delinquency, the CAP developed recreation programs such as summer camps for neighborhood children that took place in community areas such as police and church buildings (Kobrin 1966). Community improvement also was a focus of the CAP, and local schools, sanitation departments, and police units were examined to see how these services could be enhanced. The CAP also attempted to help those who had already became involved in delinquent and criminal behavior. Delinquency prevention was accomplished by developing strategies for the courts and police when supervising delinquent youth, setting up visits for those in detention, working with juvenile gangs, as well as helping adult parolees to get situated once they returned to their communities (Kobrin 1966).

South Chicago has changed little since the days when the CAP was first implemented (Schlossman, Zellman, and Shavelson 1984). The community is still impoverished and with few job opportunities; however, the racial composition of the neighborhood has changed. In 1934 South Chicago was primarily Polish, and this group is whom the CAP programs targeted. Fifty years later, the majority population was Mexican, with a significant number of African Americans. CAP programs were heavily tied to the Polish community, so as the makeup of the community gradually changed, the CAP programs eventually shut down in the late 1950s. In the 1960s, however, new programs that relied on the philosophies of the CAP began to develop in the Mexican and African American communities. These programs were developed and implemented by local community leaders and then funded by the CAP (Schlossman, Zellman, and Shavelson 1984).

The CAP was one of the first attempts at preventing and treating delinquent behavior in the inner city. Evaluations show that the CAP programs helped build community coherence and decrease delinquency (Schlossman, Zellman, and Shavelson 1984; *V.I.P. Examiner* 1991). However, the CAP evaluations have not been methodologically sound, and so one cannot necessarily conclude that the CAP was a success until further research is conducted. The CAP did influence delinquency prevention, and its effect can be seen today in community-based recreation programs such as Boys & Girls Clubs and in mentor programs like Big Brothers Big Sisters of America.

One way to tackle crime prevention is through community-based programs such as Head Start, a preschool program that targets economically disadvantaged and at-risk children (www.nhsa.org 2004). This program began in the early 1960s as part of President Lyndon Johnson's War on Poverty, and it combines quality preschool education with parent education. One particular Head Start program, the Perry Preschool Project, was developed in Ypsilanti, Michigan, in 1962 and targeted poor, at-risk African American children (Berrueta 1987). The children who participated in the program for one to two years had half as many arrests and were more likely to graduate from high school and go on to college or vocational school than children who did not participate (Berrueta 1987). Because of recent economic downturns, however, Head Start is at risk for losing funding in many areas (www.nhsa.org 2004).

A second type of community-based crime prevention program is a mentor program. Such programs identify youth who are at risk and match them with mentors or responsible adults from the community (Brown and Henriques 1997). The mentors volunteer a few hours a month of their time to spend time with the children they have been matched with. Big Brothers Big Sisters of America is one mentor program that has been deemed successful. One evaluation of this program found that children involved in Big Brothers Big Sisters were less likely to use drugs or alcohol or to hit another child in comparison to children who were not involved in the program (Tierney, Grossman, and Resch 1995). This study also found that children in Big Brothers Big Sisters improved their grades in school as well as relationships with peers and family.

After-school programs also are an important part of community-based prevention because many children are often home alone between the time school lets out and when their parent(s) arrive home. This time period is when children are the most likely to get into trouble. After-school programs provide children with a supervised, safe place to go, where they can get help with homework or participate in recreational activities. Evaluations of these programs show that children involved in after-school programs are less likely to use drugs, be arrested, or engage in delinquent behavior (Welsh and Hoshi 2001).

There are many after-school programs for children. One such program, Blossoms, in Brooklyn, New York, targets girls between the ages of twelve and fifteen who are at risk for gang activity (www.npr.org/programs/atc/ 2003). The founder of the program, Isis Sapp-Grant, is a former girl gang leader who, after receiving her master's degree in social work, started Blossoms as a way to give back to her community. Parents, the school, or the district attorney's office referred the girls in this program for delinquent behavior such as not attending school or fighting. The girls live in impoverished neighborhoods where gang activity is the norm. Blossoms teaches the girls the dangers of gangs and how to stay away from them; at the same time the girls receive mentoring and encouragement to achieve their dreams. Girls who complete the program attend a graduation ceremony and receive a certificate of leadership (www.npr.org/programs/atc/ 2003).

Another after-school program that targets at-risk children is the Council for Unity. Robert De Sena started Council for Unity in 1975, and there are currently fifty-five programs in the United States; the majority of programs are based in the state of New York (www.npr.org/programs/atc/ 2003). The Council for Unity focuses on children in impoverished neighborhoods who are at risk for serious delinquency and possible gang activity. This program teaches high school youth ways to manage situations without resorting to violence and how to stay out of gangs. The Council for Unity has had great success: 96 percent of its members graduate from high school, and of those who graduate, an additional 97 percent go on to college (www.npr.org/programs/atc/ 2003).

Community-based crime prevention programs such as Head Start, Big Brothers Big Sisters of America, and after-school programs have been successful in reducing delinquent behavior and promoting positive social skills. These types of programs allow for early involvement in the life of an at-risk child and thus reduce the chances that the child will become delinquent.

Many leading sociologists (for example, William Julius Wilson) have concluded that the underlying causes of many of our social ills must be the focus of intervention efforts if we are to achieve real and lasting success. We concur with Krisberg and Austin (1993), who call for a new generation of child savers. However, it seems unlikely that real social change in the manner suggested by sociologists will be implemented in this current political climate that emphasizes individual responsibility (and thus punishment).

Still, we agree with Samuel Walker (2001, 290) when he asserts, "Experts in criminal justice have a professional obligation to search for the truth and to speak the truth, even though most people would prefer not to hear it." Our best understanding of the truth is contained within the pages of this book. Our response to the important question, "What should we do about juvenile justice?" is this: we should recommit ourselves to the welfare of young people. While we acknowledge that accountability and responsibility are vitally important, we believe there is a tremendous need to recommit ourselves to caring for and nurturing young people, even when they disappoint and sometimes frighten us with their behavior.

We summarize the promising and possible solutions to delinquency in Table 2.3, by listing several dos and don'ts. We call for more treatment, more efforts toward prevention, and considerably less emphasis on incarceration and punishment. We agree with Richard Lundman (2001, 298) and others who argue that there are basically three groups of juvenile offenders

Table 2.3
Summary of Recommendations

Do	Don't
Emphasize early prevention	Rely heavily on incarceration or institutionalized treatment
Focus prevention efforts on the most at-risk youth and communities	Transfer nonviolent offenders to the adult criminal justice system
Provide intensive probation for juveniles involved in serious property crime	Place status offenders on probation or send them to juvenile institutions
Divert as many status offenders and other minor, nonviolent offenders as quickly as possible	Use Scared Straight, boot camp, or other shock-type programs
	Rely on traditional treatment programs that focus on the individual offender
Provide intensive treatment that treats the entire family and focuses on multiple problems (e.g., education, substance abuse, peer relations)	Abandon the original goals of the juvenile court, but find ways to improve treatment and prevention

with which society must contend. Each group has different needs and requires different responses:

1. Status and minor offenders: This is a very large group of offenders. Most of these youth will mature and grow up and out of delinquent behavior. They should be diverted from the system as quickly as possible. We should avoid labeling and stigmatizing them. They should not be placed in the company of hard-core offenders.

2. Moderately delinquent offenders: A somewhat smaller group of offenders than status and minor offenders. These youth tend to engage in drug and property crimes, but they are not violent. They should receive probation and other forms of community treatment. Innovative treatment programs (like MST) should be court ordered. Restorative justice programs can be

fruitfully used with this group. Most important, offenders in this group should not be incarcerated.

3. Chronic few: This is the smallest group of all, the violent and chronic few who are responsible for a disproportionate share of violent crime. These youthful offenders should be placed into secure treatment programs (i.e., incarcerated) until they demonstrate that they are no longer violent and a threat to society. Those violent and chronic few not able or willing to change their behavior should be waived to the adult criminal justice system. Society deserves to be protected from these hard-core offenders.

A Note on Juvenile Gangs

Juvenile gangs have been around a long time in the United States, dating back at least to the nineteenth century. Not all juvenile gangs, of course, can be considered delinquent gangs, a point noted by some of the earliest studies of gangs in the United States, such as the important study of over 1,000 gangs in Chicago by Frederick Thrasher in the 1920s (Thrasher 1927). Many juvenile gangs do become delinquent groups, however, and they can have serious consequences for the neighborhoods in which they reside. This section will discuss some issues related to delinquent youth gangs.

Over the years, there have been numerous private and public efforts to eliminate, or at least reduce, gang activity throughout the country. Despite these efforts, however, juvenile gangs continue to exist in many major cities and have been encroaching into suburban areas and smaller towns for several decades. From the 1970s through the 1990s, for example, surveys of gangs estimated that there was an "explosion" in the growth of gangs throughout the United States, particularly in small and medium-sized communities (Curry and Decker, 2003, 27). Some surveys suggest that the growth of gangs in the United States peaked around the middle of the 1990s. David Curry and Scott Decker, for example, present data that show that the number of gangs peaked in 1996, with an estimated 30,818 gangs. The following year, there were an estimated 30,533 gangs in the United States, and by 2000, the estimated number of gangs had dropped to 24,742 (Curry and Decker 2003, 28).

Concern about gangs has even spread into American Indian communities. Studies indicate that American Indian and Alaska Native populations have a higher crime rate than the U.S. population overall and that their violent crime rate is especially high. Researchers suggest that an important factor in the high levels of crime and violence in these communities is the increase of youth gang activity. These criminal behaviors were not reflected in previous estimates of delinquency and youth gang activity because tribal police and leadership contacts have not always been included in surveys and studies of gangs. These recent surveys and studies of delinquency in American Indian populations suggest that the pattern of gang delinquency in these areas is similar to that of gangs in other parts of the country; however, the problems with American Indian youth gangs began in the mid-1990s (Major et al. 2002). Also, efforts to control or reduce gang activity in American Indian areas are similar to those efforts used for other gangs, some of which are described below. In particular, American Indian youth gangs are being treated with preventive efforts such as school-based programs and suppression techniques, which tend to focus on greater law enforcement surveillance and activity.

While some of the theoretical ideas and treatment-intervention programs mentioned earlier are applicable to gangs as well as individual juveniles, other efforts focus on gangs either primarily or exclusively. For example, the Chicago Area Project (see earlier) was developed in the 1930s largely as an anti-gang effort. In the 1960s government programs focused on economic incentives as an important means of combating gang activity and growth in major U.S. cities. In the late 1960s and early 1970s, gangs were thought to have declined in the United States, and some felt that this decline in gang activity was the result of gang prevention programs. Since the late 1970s, however, it has become apparent that gangs continue to exist and may even be more dangerous than in the past. As mentioned earlier, gangs have become a regular part of most urban landscapes, even emerging in areas where they previously were rarely seen, such as small towns and suburbs (Siegel and Senna 2000, chap. 9).

Many gang prevention programs have included the use of forceful police intervention, identifying gang members or potential members of gangs and arresting them. The arrest of gang members as a major anti-gang response is often coupled with more punitive legislation, designed to deter potential gang activity and membership with the threat of increased punishment for gang-related criminal behavior. This practice has been called the "suppression" method, and it is one of the more popular methods of gang prevention (Bartollas 2003).

In 2003 and 2004, for example, the attorney general of Virginia convened a task force to combat growing gang involvement in the state's major metropolitan areas and even in some smaller cities. The major result of the task force's findings was a request by the attorney general to increase punishments for gang-related crimes. There was also a call for greater gang prevention efforts, especially using the resources of Boys & Girls Clubs, but the major thrust seemed to be more punitive legislation aimed at gang behavior.

Some are beginning to realize, however, that suppression is not the only answer to gang prevention, and may not even be the most effective way of dealing with gangs. In recognition of the multiple causes of gangs, some communities are supporting environmental programs. One example of such a program is a project called Gang Resistance Education and Training, or G.R.E.A.T. G.R.E.A.T. is considered a primary prevention program because it is focused on youth in the community, as opposed to youngsters who are considered at high risk for gang involvement or are already members of gangs. G.R.E.A.T. began in Phoenix, Arizona, in 1991. It is offered in middle school settings, especially to students in grades six and seven. G.R.E.A.T. involves police officers who go into the schools and teach an eight- or nine-week course on good behavior, peer relationships, and similar conformist concepts. Evaluations of G.R.E.A.T. programs yield mixed reviews. Most evaluations conclude that the program works to prevent future gang involvement in youth who have been exposed to the principles of the G.R.E.A.T. program, but the effects are negligible (Curry and Decker 2003; Shelden, Tracy, and Brown 2001; Esbensen 2000).

Another gang prevention strategy is called GRP, or Gang Reduction Program (*OJJDP News at a Glance* 2003). GRP is an experimental program currently being piloted in four U.S. cities: Los Angeles, California; Milwaukee, Wisconsin; Richmond, Virginia; and Miami, Florida. It is sponsored by the Office of Juvenile Justice and Delinquency Prevention (OJJDP) within the U.S. Department of Justice. The goals of GRP are to reduce youth gangs and gang-related violence in certain neighborhoods in the pilot communities. It includes primary prevention, involving youth in general, as well as other intervention strategies aimed at juvenile gang members or potential gang members. GRP is considered more comprehensive than other gang reduction or gang prevention programs because it includes families of gang members and at-risk youth as well as the youth themselves. In addition, GRP identifies and responds to community needs, such as recreational and financial needs, in an effort to prevent gangs from becoming attractive to young people. GRP also expends considerable effort toward identifying suitable alternatives to gang membership. Thus it may follow suppression with efforts and strategies for successful reintegration of former gang members into the community (*OJJDP News at a Glance* 2003).

The Comprehensive Community-Wide Approach to Gang Prevention, Intervention, and Suppression is another community gang prevention effort (Bartollas 2003, 316). It is based on a model introduced in Chicago and now used in several communities throughout the country, such as Bloomington, Illinois; Tucson and Mesa, Arizona; Riverside, California; and San Antonio, Texas. As the title of this program indicates, it is a multifaceted and comprehensive approach to the reduction of gang activity in an area. This program uses efforts to prevent youth from joining gangs in the first place, but it also uses more aggressive efforts to intervene with youth who are already members of gangs. Early evaluations of this program indicate that gang-related criminal activity and gang memberships are reduced in those communities where it has been implemented, but it is too early to say if these reactions are stable and truly attributable to the effectiveness of the program. What the overall assessments of this program do indicate, however, is that true reductions in gang activities should be multidimensional or integrated and should include not only law enforcement activity but also efforts from other parts of a community or neighborhood, such as schools, families, churches, and the business community. In addition, the results of this program suggest that early intervention efforts—for example, in elementary school—are important in the prevention of gang involvement (Bartollas 2003, 316).

Evaluations of these gang prevention programs indicate that they show some promise in reducing gang membership and the allure of gang involvement for youth whose lives are not well integrated into conventional family and school activities. It is now known, however, that no single gang intervention strategy can be effective for all types of gangs and in all communities. Gangs offer youngsters a life of excitement and easy money, and many prevention programs find it hard to teach kids to resist that kind of temptation. Still, anti-gang efforts continue to develop wherever gangs exist or may potentially develop. Many communities have created at least modestly successful programs for preventing some youth from joining gangs. Suppression efforts are successful at getting particularly troublesome gang members off the street, at least for a while. However, gangs continue to appear, even in neighborhoods that have previously eliminated them, in part because the social and economic reasons for gang membership are still attractive to many youth. That situation will be difficult to change without a change in the social circumstances and conditions that give rise to the temptations of gangs to those who are young and impressionable.

Conclusion

In this chapter, we have made several important points: (1) U.S. society is critical of juvenile justice but not sure of how best to improve it (this is the identity crisis we spoke of); (2) delinquency is a complex matter, so effective solutions must be comprehensive and multifaceted; (3) there are numerous problems facing juvenile justice, some of the most important of which are an overwhelmed system with limited resources and a serious and growing overrepresentation of minority and poor youth; and (4) there appear to be promising ways to improve juvenile justice and prevent delinquency, so abandoning the system at this time seems unwise (and unlikely).

We have also provided a number of suggestions, based on social science evidence, on how best to reform the juvenile justice system. We argue that only violent juvenile offenders, who make up a small percentage of delinquent youth, should be placed in secure institutions. Most juvenile offenders are better off diverted from the system (in the case of status offenders and minor offenders) or placed on probation and given appropriate community-based intervention (such as restorative justice programs for moderately delinquent youth).

While we have been critical of many juvenile justice efforts, policies, and programs, we wish to acknowledge that most of the employees in the juvenile justice system—as best as we can tell from our research and our own personal experiences—are dedicated professionals who genuinely desire to help troubled youth. Day in and day out they work in jobs that are often stressful. They likely have, at best, modest—at worst, shamelessly low—incomes, and they don't get the recognition and appreciation they deserve. We applaud their efforts and dedication, and we simply offer our best insights and suggestions so that more youth, families, and communities can receive the help they need. After all, we are all in this together.

References

Acoca, Leslie. 2004. "Outside/Inside: The Violation of American Girls at Home, on the Streets, and in the Juvenile Justice System." Pp. 77-96 in Meda Chesney-Lind and Lisa Pasko, eds., *Girls, Women and Crime: Selected Readings*. Thousand Oaks, CA: Sage.

Armstrong, Gaylene S., Angela R. Gover, and Doris L. MacKenzie. 2002. "The Development and Diversity of Correctional Boot Camps." In *Turnstile Justice: Issues in American Corrections*, 2nd ed. Upper Saddle River, NJ: Prentice-Hall.

Bartollas, Clemens. 1997. *Juvenile Delinquency*, 4th ed. New York: Allyn and Bacon.

———. 2003. *Juvenile Delinquency*, 6th ed. New York: Allyn and Bacon.

Bazemore, Gordon. 2001. "Young People, Trouble, and Crime: Restorative Justice as a Normative Theory of Informal Social Control and Social Support." *Youth and Society* 33: 199–226.

Bazemore, Gordon, and Mark S. Umbreit. 1994. *Balanced and Restorative Justice: Program Summary*. Washington, DC: Office of Juvenile Justice and Delinquency Prevention.

———. 2001. *A Comparison of Four Restorative Conferencing Models*. Washington, DC: Office of Juvenile Justice and Delinquency Prevention.

Beckett, Kathy, and Theodore Sasson. 2000. *The Politics of Injustice: Crime and Punishment in America*. Thousand Oaks, CA: Pine Forge.

Belenko, Steven. 2001. *Research on Drug Courts: A Critical Review, 2001 Update*. Alexandria, VA: National Drug Court Institute.

Berger, Ronald J., ed. 1996. *The Sociology of Juvenile Delinquency*, 2nd ed. Chicago: Nelson-Hall.

Berrueta, Clement John R. 1987. "The Effects of Early Educational Intervention on Crime and Delinquency in Adolescence and Early Adulthood." Pp. 220–240 in John D. Burchard and Sara Burchard, eds., *Prevention of Delinquent Behavior.* Newbury Park, CA: Sage.

Bishop, Donna M., Charles E. Frazier, Lonn Lanza-Kaduce, and Lawrence Winner. 1996. "The Transfer of Juveniles to Criminal Court: Does It Make a Difference?" *Crime and Delinquency* 42: 171–191.

Braithwaite, John. 1989. *Crime, Shame, and Reintegration.* New York: Cambridge University Press.

Brown, Delores D., and Zelma Weston Henriques. 1997. *"Promises and Pitfalls of Mentoring as a Juvenile Justice Strategy."* Social Justice 24: 212–234.

Butts, Jeffrey A., Janeen Buck, and Mark B. Coggeshall. 2002. *The Impact of Teen Court on Young Offenders.* Washington, DC: Urban Institute.

California Department of Youth Authority. 1997. "LEAD: A Boot Camp and Intensive Parole Program. The Final Impact Evaluation." Available online at www.cya.ca.gov/contact/reports.html.

Cox, Steven M., and John J. Conrad. 1996. *Juvenile Justice: A Guide to Practice and Theory,* 4th ed. Madison, WI: Brown & Benchmark.

Curry, G. David, and Scott H. Decker. 2003. *Confronting Gangs: Crime and Community,* 2nd ed. Los Angeles: Roxbury.

Drug Court Standards Committee. 1997. *Defining Drug Courts: The Key Components.* Washington, DC: U.S. Department of Justice, Office of Justice Programs.

Esbensen, Finn-Aage. 2000. "Preventing Adolescent Gang Involvement." *Juvenile Justice Bulletin,* September. Washington, DC: U.S. Department of Justice, Office of Juvenile Justice and Delinquency Prevention.

Freeman-Wilson, Judge Karen, Ronald Sullivan, and Susan P. Weinstein. 2003. *Critical Issues for Defense Attorneys in Drug Court.* Monograph Series 4. Alexandria, VA: National Drug Court Institute.

Garbarino, James. 1999. *Lost Boys: Why Our Sons Turn Violent and How We Can Help Them.* New York: Free Press.

Harrison, Paige, James R. Maupin, and G. Larry Mays. 2001. "Teen Court: An Examination of Processes and Outcomes." *Crime and Delinquency* 47: 243–264.

Hay, Carter. 2001. "An Exploratory Test of Braithwaite's Reintegrative Shaming Theory." *Youth and Society* 38: 132–153.

Hubner, John, and Jill Wolfson. 1996. *Somebody Else's Children: The Courts, the Kids, and the Struggle to Save America's Troubled Families.* New York: Crown.

Inciardi, James A. 2002. *Criminal Justice,* 7th ed. Belmont, CA: Wadsworth.

Kobrin, Solomon. 1966. "The Chicago Area Project—A Twenty-five Year Assessment." Pp. 473–482 in Rose Giallombardo, ed., *Juvenile Delinquency.* New York: John Wiley and Sons.

Krisberg, B., and J. F. Austin. 1993. *Reinventing Juvenile Justice.* Newbury Park, CA: Sage.

Lockwood, Dorothy, Jill McCorkel, and James Inciardi. 1998. "Developing Comprehensive Prison-based Therapeutic Community Treatment for Women." *Drugs and Society* 13: 193–212.

Lundman, Richard J. 2001. *Prevention and Control of Juvenile Delinquency,* 3rd ed. New York: Oxford University Press.

Lynch, Frank. 1970. "Social Acceptance Reconsidered." Pp. 1–63 in Frank Lynch and Alfronso de Guzman, II, eds., *Four Readings on Philippine Values,* 3rd ed. Quezon City, Philippines: Ateneo de Manila University.

Lynch, Frank, and Alfronso de Guzman, II, eds. 1973. *Four Readings on Philippine Values,* 4th ed. Quezon City, Philippines: Ateneo de Manila University.

MacKenzie, Doris L., and Andre Rosay. 1996. "Correctional Boot Camps for Juveniles." P. xx in *Juvenile and Adult Boot Camps.* Laurel, MD: American Correctional Association.

Major, Aline K., Arlen Egley, Jr., James C. Howell, Barbara Mendenhall, and Troy Armstrong. 2002. "Youth Gangs in Indian Country." *Juvenile Justice Bulletin,* March. Washington, DC: U.S. Department of Justice, Office of Juvenile Justice and Delinquency Prevention.

Martin, Steve S., Clifford Butzin, Christine Saum, and James A. Inciardi. 1996. "Three-Year Outcomes of Therapeutic Community Treatment for Drug-involved Offenders in Delaware: From Prison to Work Release to After Care." *The Prison Journal* 79: 294–320.

Martinson, Robert. 1974. "What Works?—Questions and Answers about Prison Reform." *The Public Interest* 35: 22–54.

McCold, Paul. 1999. "Restorative Justice Practice—The State of the Field 1999." International Institute for Restorative Practices. Available online at http://www.iirp.org/library/vt/vt_mccold.html.

Miller, Jerome G. 1991. *Last One over the Wall: The Massachusetts Experiment in Closing Reform Schools.* Columbus: Ohio State University Press.

———. 1996. *Search and Destroy: African-American Males in the Criminal Justice System.* Cambridge: Cambridge University Press.

Minor, Kevin I., James B. Wells, and Irina R. Soderstrom. 1999. "Sentence Completion and Recidivism among Juveniles Referred to Teen Courts." *Crime and Delinquency* 45: 467–480.

National Head Start Association. 2002. Available online at http://www.nhsa.org.

Office of Juvenile Justice and Delinquency Prevention. 1998. "Guide for Implementing the Balanced and Restorative Justice Model." Available online at www.ojjdp.ncjrs.org/pubs/implementing/contents.html.

———. 1999. "OJJDP Research: Making a Difference for Juveniles." Available online at www.ojjdp.ncjrs.org/pubs/makingadiffer/contents.html.

Ohlin, Lloyd E., Alden D. Miller, and Robert B. Coates. n.d. *Juvenile Correctional Reform in Massachusetts: A Preliminary Report of the Center for Criminal Justice of the Harvard Law School.* Washington, DC: U.S. Government Printing Office.

OJJDP News at a Glance. 2003. Washington, DC: U.S. Department of Justice, Office of Juvenile Justice and Delinquency Prevention, September/October, vol. II, no. 5.

Robinson, Kenneth D. 2000. "Research Update: Reports on Recent Drug Court Research." *National Drug Court Institute Review* 1: 121–134.

Schlossman, Steven, Gail Zellman, and Richard Shavelson. 1984. *Delinquency Prevention in South Chicago: A Fifty-Year Assessment of the Chicago Area Project.* Santa Monica, CA: Rand.

Shelden, Randall G., Sharon K. Tracy, and William B. Brown. 2001. *Youth Gangs in American Society,* 2nd ed. Belmont, CA: Wadsworth/Thomson Learning.

Siegel, Larry. 2002. *Juvenile Delinquency: The Core.* Belmont, CA: Wadsworth.

Siegel, Larry, and Joseph Senna. 2000. *Juvenile Delinquency: Theory, Practice, and Law,* 7th ed. Belmont, CA: Wadsworth.

Snyder, H., T. Finnegan, W. Kang, R. Poole, A. Stahl, and Y. Wan. 2001. "Easy Access to Juvenile Court Statistics: 1989–1998." Available online at http://ojjdp.ncjrs.org/ojstatbb/ezajcs98.

Snyder, Howard N., and Melissa Sickmund. 1999. *Juvenile Offenders and Victims: 1999 National Report.* Washington, DC: Office of Juvenile Justice and Delinquency Prevention.

Thrasher, Frederick M. 1927. *The Gang.* Chicago: University of Chicago Press.

Tierney, Joseph P., Jean Baldwin Grossman, and Nancy L. Resch. 1995. *Making a Difference: An Impact Study of Big Brothers/Big Sisters.* Philadelphia: Public/Private Ventures.

University of Maryland. 1997. *Preventing Crime: What Works, What Doesn't, What's Promising.* Washington, DC: U.S. Government Printing Office.

V.I.P. Examiner. 1991. "Chicago Area Project: A Delinquency Prevention Model." *V.I.P. Examiner* (Summer): 6–11, 14–17.

Walker, Samuel. 2001. *Sense and Nonsense about Crime and Drugs: A Policy Guide,* 5th ed. Belmont, CA: Wadsworth.

Welsh, Brandon C., and Akemi Hoshi. 2001. "Communities and Crime Prevention." Pp. 165–197 in Lawrence W. Sherman, David P. Farrington, Brandon C. Welsh, and Doris Layton MacKenzie, eds., *Evidence-based Crime Prevention.* New York: Routledge.

Wexler, Henry K. 1995. "The Success of Therapeutic Communities for Substance Abusers in American Prisons." *Journal of Psychoactive Drugs* 27: 57–66.

Wexler, Henry K., G. P. Falkin, and Douglas S. Lipton. 1988. *A Model Prison Rehabilitation Program: An Evaluation of the Stay'n Out Therapeutic Community.* A Final Report to the National Institute on Drug Abuse. Washington, DC: National Institute of Justice.

Whitehead, John T., and Steven P. Lab. 1999. *Juvenile Justice: An Introduction,* 3rd ed. Cincinnati, OH: Anderson.

Winner, Lawrence, Lonn Lanza-Kaduce, Donna Bishop, and Charles E. Frazier. 1996. "The Transfer of Juveniles to Criminal Court: Reexamining Recidivism over the Long Term." *Crime and Delinquency* 43: 548–563.

Zehner, Sharon J. 1997. "Teen Court." *FBI Law Enforcement Bulletin* 66: 1–7.

Zhang, Sheldon X. 2000. *Evaluation of the Los Angeles County Juvenile Drug Treatment Boot Camp: Executive Summary.* Washington, DC: National Institute of Justice.

Web Sources

www.law.cornell.edu

This is a good source for current information on U.S. Supreme Court case decisions. The cases are usually summarized but include relevant facts and arguments, including majority and minority opinions.

www.npr.org/programs/atc/

This link will take you directly to the Web page for All Things Considered. The radio broadcast specifically mentioned in this chapter is titled "From Rubies to Gems" and was aired in February 2003.

3

Chronology

The following list includes important milestones and events in the development of juvenile justice institutions, concepts and practices, and legal rights in the United States. This information is addressed and referenced in other chapters, but the material is presented here in chronological order. The lists are divided into several topical areas and are listed chronologically within each of these topics. A summary of these concepts, programs, and court decisions is provided in Table 3.1 (page 103).

It will be apparent to the reader that the philosophies and goals of projects move from treatment to punishment and back to treatment again over the course of several decades, for more than 200 years. This kind of vacillation in programs and philosophies is common for juvenile justice projects. As a society, the United States, like all other countries, is not in total agreement on the best way to handle, prevent, or even reduce delinquent behavior. In part, this indecision is caused by the many kinds of delinquent acts that can be committed, from murder to minor forms of violations, such as status offenses.

In addition, the whole juvenile justice system was once regarded as a kind of experiment, one that is now over 100 years old but still attracts very different reactions, from total acceptance to almost total denial. While some may call for a total revamping of juvenile courts and correctional institutions, others argue that the only real way to deal with youthful offenders is to place them into a separate system of courts, institutions, and treatment specialists, in short, the juvenile justice system as we know it today. Whichever philosophical stance one takes on this subject, it is clear that we are still searching for better solutions to the problem of delinquency and that the search will not be over anytime in the near future. In the meantime, all we can really do in this matter is to keep looking for good ways to handle our young people's difficulties with life and to try to make their lives better and our country all the stronger in the process.

The Development of Juvenile Correctional Institutions in the United States

1817   The **Society for the Prevention of Pauperism** is formed in New York. This organization tries to eliminate or control poverty and its associated conditions, such as immigration, gambling, prostitution, and public drunkenness. Its efforts eventually lead to the opening of the first house of refuge in 1825, in New York. In 1824, the society becomes known as the Society for the Reformation of Juvenile Delinquents.

1825   The **New York House of Refuge** opens, the first public institution for youthful offenders in the United States. It is based on the model of rehabilitation through work and discipline. Other houses of refuge are established throughout the eastern seaboard and in the Midwest through the middle of the nineteenth century.

1846   **Lyman School for Boys,** the first public juvenile correctional institution, or reformatory, in the United States, opens in Westborough, Massachusetts. Many of these early institutions are referred to as "industrial schools," and they are large, impersonal juvenile prisons. Some later adopt the name "training schools," but all of these institutions are places where juvenile offenders are confined for rehabilitation and punishment.

1856   The **cottage system** is introduced into juvenile corrections with the establishment of the **State Industrial School for Girls** in Lancaster, Massachusetts. The cottage system emphasizes the creation of a family-like atmosphere within a correctional institution, including the hiring of cottage parents as supervisors for youthful inmates. It is commonly used in earlier institutions, and it is still used in many juvenile correctional facilities today.

1889   **Hull-House**, a settlement facility for immigrant families, is founded in Chicago. It provides a variety of social and legal services for these families, including protective associations for immigrants and their children, citizenship training, recreational opportunities, psychological services, educational and job assistance, and cultural enrichment opportunities and activities.

1890s   **Detention centers** are first established. Detention centers, or detention halls, are holding facilities for juvenile offenders who are awaiting a hearing in juvenile court. In addition, they may house juvenile offenders who have been found delinquent in juvenile court but are waiting transfer to a juvenile correctional institution. They operate much like jails, but they deal with juvenile defendants instead of adults. Their primary purpose is to maintain custody and control of juveniles awaiting juvenile court hearings or transfers to other juvenile institutions. If there is no detention center available to juveniles, they will likely be sent to a local jail for the same purpose as the detention center. When juveniles are placed in a jail, however, they need to be separated from adults in the jail.

1900–   **Child-guidance clinics** are established as support units
1920   for juvenile courts. Some of these clinics are large, and their mission is to treat juveniles referred to them by the courts. These clinics are an example of the medical model, which adheres to the philosophy of juvenile courts at the turn of the twentieth century. Most of them emphasize individualized treatment based on psychiatric or psychological counseling.

1960s– **Halfway houses and group homes** are created. These
1970s   are quasi-supervised settings, and residents go to school or to work during the day. One example is a group home established in Silverlake, California, where public education and group counseling are emphasized. Resi-

1960s– dents are allowed to attend public schools in California
1970s, but are given intensive group counseling at the home.
cont. Other similar programs are the **Criswell House**, in
Florida, which also emphasizes group treatment, and
the **Dare Project** in Massachusetts. In the 1970s, Florida
establishes several group homes based on the Criswell
House model. The Dare system in Massachusetts involves specialized group homes and treatment facilities
within an overall system of treatment and specialized
care for youthful offenders.

The **House of Umoja** in Philadelphia is another example of a treatment-oriented group home program. The
Umoja system emphasizes cultural identity for African
American gang youth and stresses nonviolence and cultural pride as means of stemming gang delinquency
among its residents. Not all group homes offer organized and specialized treatment services. In some, juveniles are kept for longer periods of stay than would be
the case if they had been confined in traditional institutional settings.

1970s **Day treatment**, or nonresidential, programs are established. Day treatment involves providing services to
youth who are allowed to stay at home and go to school
but who must report to the treatment center during
specified periods. These programs are often much
cheaper to operate than correctional institutions are,
and they offer opportunities for parental involvement
and other community-based inputs in the overall treatment plan for juveniles. Day treatment centers are especially popular in California and New York, but they exist in most states. A successful example of a
nonresidential program is the **Associated Marine Insti-
tutes (AMI),** which has over forty schools throughout
the United States. A major emphasis in these schools is
obtaining a high school equivalent degree (GED) or getting as much education as possible. In addition, youth
are exposed to life skills training, such as first aid and
lifesaving, as well as ocean-related job training, including ship handling, scuba diving (where juveniles may

earn a certificate), marine photography, and related skills and activities. Youth are asked to sign a contract before entering the program and are expected to continue school or to enroll in military service upon completing the program. Follow-up assistance is given to graduates for three years beyond completion of the AMI program.

Project New Pride is another example of a nonresidential program. The program begins in Denver, Colorado, and spreads to several other states in the 1970s. Project New Pride caters to minority youth and tries to instill in them a sense of pride and self-worth. The total treatment program usually lasts one year and emphasizes cultural pride, academic success, and job training.

Similar nonresidential programs that focus on education, survival skills, and job training are **Outward Bound** and **Vision Quest**. Both programs emphasize learning self-reliance skills through activities such as mountain climbing, canoeing, desert hiking, and survival at sea. Vision Quest also offers a wagon train experience for its youth.

Nonresidential programs continue to offer alternative treatment and basic needs services to delinquent youth, but their popularity, especially as day treatment centers, declines in the next ten to fifteen years.

1972   The juvenile correctional system in Massachusetts is closed under the direction of **Jerome Miller**. Miller decides to close these institutions after several years of reform efforts are tried and found to be ineffective. Thirty years later, Massachusetts remains one of the few states without a system of juvenile correctional institutions in place. Instead, the state has developed a contract system whereby representatives of juvenile corrections in Massachusetts review bids for placements and services from public and private agencies and organizations and oversee their contractual agreements for the care and treatment of juvenile offenders.

1980s   **Boot camps** for juvenile offenders are opened in the United States. Often considered a form of probation for juveniles found delinquent of criminal or delinquent offenses, boot camps can also be used as the only form of punishment or treatment of youthful offenders. They typically involve a few months of confinement under strict living conditions, similar to the boot camp experience in the military, followed by a few months of supervision and monitoring in the community. In the 1990s, other boot camp models are developed, some with more success than the traditional, harsh discipline of earlier, military-style models.

1990s–
present   The use of institutions for punishment and treatment increases, although the length of stay per confinement continues to decline. Alternatives to institutions are becoming popular, such as **restorative justice**, which focuses on the offender meeting the victim, members of the victim's family, and other individuals in the community's juvenile justice system. One goal of restorative justice programs is that those involved in the case agree that the offender is properly remorseful or sorrowful for his or her actions and that the victim, and sometimes others related to the victim, are satisfied with the outcome of the case. Thus, a sense of peace and justice is thought to be restored within the community or at least between the offender and the victim.

Ideas, Events, and Programs

Middle
Ages   Juveniles are treated like small adults, with little or no distinction by age for responsibility for criminal acts.

1500s   **Poor laws** are established in England. These laws support the apprenticeship of idle and wayward juveniles to craftsmen and skilled workers so that they can learn a trade instead of turning to thievery and crime.

1500–
1600   The idea that children are different from adults begins to appear in literature. Thus, the concept of **childhood** begins to develop.

1764   *On Crimes and Punishment,* by Cesare Beccaria, is published. This book becomes the source of what is known as the classical school, which promotes punishment of adults and children alike for criminal behavior. Beccaria's philosophy is thus consistent with the view that children are little more than miniature adults. However, the classical school also supports punishment in moderation. The death penalty, for example, is not a significant part of this philosophy of criminal justice.

Late   The idea of childhood as a separate social and legal sta-
1700s   tus begins to influence laws and policy makers in Europe and America. Children are seen as needing nurturing and treatment instead of punishment. Special programs and institutions are thought to be necessary to provide this nurturing and treatment. One of the first visible results of this emerging philosophy is the establishment of houses of refuge, starting with the New York House of Refuge in 1825.

1841   John Augustus, often called the "father of probation," initiates the first **probation** program, in Boston. Probation entails supervising and working with convicted criminals in the community instead of sending these offenders to a prison or correctional institution. Augustus is a shoemaker by trade and has no training for supervising and counseling criminal offenders, yet he makes great strides in promoting the usefulness and success of probation. Augustus not only helps juveniles find work, but he also tries to get educational training or additional schooling for those youth assigned to him. Over several decades, Augustus is responsible for the supervision and correction of over 2,000 juvenile and adult offenders. Probation becomes an official policy of correctional programs, first in Massachusetts and then in virtually all other states, beginning in the latter part of the nineteenth century.

1853   The **Children's Aid Society (CAS)** is established in New York City by William Brace to help find temporary placements for poor, vagrant, and criminal children so they might have a better chance in life. The philosophy

1853,
cont.
of the society and its founder is that children need nurturing and loving-kindness in order to become successful
adults and citizens. Some think this organization and similar arrangements, such as **placing out**, are the forerunners to the modern concept of foster care. In 1890 the CAS
in Pennsylvania creates a foster home for criminal youth
to be used in place of a juvenile correctional facility.

Criminal and neglected youth who are placed out are
sent to families living in rural areas to learn useful skills
and values. These placements are more permanent than
those provided by organizations such as the CAS, so the
youth put into placing out programs may be sent away
for several years.

1869
Massachusetts passes the first **juvenile probation law**,
authorizing an employee of the state board of charities
to work on behalf of juveniles who face criminal
charges, finding them places to live and monitoring
their behavior and living conditions systematically. By
1890, probation for juveniles is a fixed part of the juvenile justice system in that state. Today, probation is the
most common disposition given to juveniles found
delinquent in juvenile courts throughout the country.
Over half of those formally adjudicated in juvenile court
are placed under some form of probation. Probation is
so common within the juvenile justice system that it is
sometimes referred to as the "workhorse" of the system,
and there are many different variations, such as intensive probation. Probation is currently considered an example of community-based corrections in most communities and states.

1874
Child abuse becomes a concern of the state in a case involving an abused girl named Mary Ellen living in New
York City. Because no laws exist to protect children in
such circumstances, the girl is eventually placed in an
orphanage, but the Society for the Prevention of Cruelty
to Children is established in New York City in 1875.

1881–
1889
In an effort to help children, states such as Michigan,
Massachusetts, and Indiana pass several acts in response to cases of neglect and child protection.

1899   The first juvenile court law, the **Illinois Juvenile Court Act,** is passed in Chicago. This law establishes a juvenile court system, as well as a probation program to be supervised by a circuit court judge, to deal with cases of crime, delinquency, dependency, and neglect (including cruelty) for youth under sixteen years of age. The law further states that no youth under the age of twelve can be placed in a jail, but any delinquent child age ten and older can be placed in the state reformatory until the age of twenty-one. The main thrust of this law is to create a nonadversarial system of justice for minors, with an emphasis on treatment and special handling instead of punishment. By 1925, juvenile courts or court systems exist in every state and in almost all jurisdictions. Some adopt the model created in 1899, while others use different models, but they all establish separate court proceedings and the philosophy of treatment over punishment.

1906   The Federation of Boys Clubs is established in Boston. In 1990, the organization changes its name to the **Boys & Girls Clubs of America (B&GCA)**. In 1994, the headquarters of the organization moves to Atlanta. There are currently over 3,000 B&GCA chapters, with programs designed to improve teen health, leadership skills, academic performance, and overall well-being, as well as gang prevention and intervention efforts.

1912   The **U.S. Children's Bureau** is created in Washington, D.C. This agency is the first federal organization established specifically to handle issues of child welfare, including the investigation of charges of abuse and mistreatment in juvenile correctional institutions.

1945–   The United States becomes concerned about gang vio-
1950   lence, especially after World War II. In New York City, investigating committees are set up to study the extent and causes of random gang violence. In response to the recommendations of the committees, the city establishes a new gang intervention policy based on the concept of the detached street worker. This position places social workers in the midst of gang territories, with the goal of interceding among warring gangs and preventing gang warfare.

1960s   The United States experiences the highest increases in delinquency in the century, particularly increased drug use and rebelliousness. In the mid-1960s, President Lyndon Johnson sponsors the creation of the Commission on Law Enforcement and the Administration of Justice to study all aspects of crime, delinquency, and crime control in the country. This commission issues a report in 1967 called *The Challenge of Crime in a Free Society.* In response to both this report and national concern over increasing crime, delinquency, and drug use, Congress passes the far-reaching **Omnibus Crime Control and Safe Streets Act** in 1968. Among other things, this act creates the **Law Enforcement Assistance Administration (LEAA)** and indirectly helps create criminal justice courses in U.S. universities and funding opportunities for criminal and juvenile justice agencies throughout the country.

1974   The U.S. Congress passes the **Juvenile Justice and Delinquency Prevention Act,** perhaps the most significant legislation involving youth since the passage of the first juvenile delinquency law in 1899. Two major goals of this act are to eliminate or alter existing status offender statutes not only within the federal jurisdiction but also among all fifty states and to reduce the population of juvenile defendants and convicted offenders in the nation's jails and correctional institutions. This act creates the **Office of Juvenile Justice and Delinquency Prevention (OJJDP),** which is responsible for funding experimental programs in the field of delinquency prevention. In 1980 LEAA is abolished and the OJJDP assumes the role of funding for juvenile justice agencies and programs throughout the country. In particular, the OJJDP focuses on alternatives to traditional institutional programs to better control and prevent delinquent behavior.

1980s   In response to "get tough" policies and successful political campaigns, beginning with the Ronald Reagan presidency, Congress and the states pass legislation that focuses on putting more juvenile offenders, especially those accused of violent and/or drug offenses, into the criminal justice system and, ultimately, into adult prisons. Consistent with this changing philosophy toward juvenile offenders, the OJJDP also begins to direct its funding efforts on those projects and programs that focus on identifying and controlling violent and repeat juvenile criminal offenders, again supporting the nation's efforts to treat these juveniles as if they were adults. Included in these programs are **boot camps** and **waivers** to the adult criminal justice system.

Boot camps are based on the philosophy that treating delinquents or predelinquents with toughness and discipline will help them reform or at least change their ways. In the 1990s, the government sponsors varying models of boot camps to try to determine which model better fits the purpose of rehabilitation and the prevention of crime.

Waivers are used to refer certain juvenile offenders to the adult criminal justice system. Some states allow juvenile court judges the discretion of sending juveniles to the adult court system, while others place this decision in the hands of the local prosecutor. Still other states permit mandatory waivers, which specify that juveniles charged with certain crimes, such as first-degree murder, be waived to the adult system automatically. In almost all states that allow waivers of juveniles to the adult criminal justice system, at least two provisions apply. First, the juvenile must be of a minimum age, typically fourteen or fifteen. Second, the crime charged must be a serious felony, such as murder or rape, but these conditions vary from state to state. One of the intended consequences of this practice is to expose juvenile offenders to long prison terms, including life imprisonment and, ultimately, the death penalty. The U.S. Supreme Court, however, rules that it is unconstitutional to execute a youth who is under the age of sixteen at the time a crime is committed. Ironically, these changes in philosophy toward more punitive measures for juvenile delinquents represent a return to the prejuvenile court days, including the Middle Ages, when children were treated as miniature adults.

1994   Congress passes the **Violent Crime Control and Law Enforcement Act**. Among other things, this act supports greater community efforts to hire police officers. It also appropriates millions of dollars to local and state efforts to control violent crime, including violent crime committed by juveniles.

1990s   Despite efforts by Congress and many state governments to become tougher and more punitive toward repeat and violent juvenile offenders, other efforts are aimed at reintegrating juvenile offenders back into the community. These **restorative justice** programs have some success, but they are still being evaluated.

Significant U.S. and State Supreme Court Decisions

1838   *Ex Parte Crouse*. This case involves a young girl sent to the Philadelphia House of Refuge for being unmanageable. In effect, the girl is confined not for a crime but instead for an act thought to be against her best interests. The girl's father complains and eventually is able to take the case to the Pennsylvania Supreme Court. The court's decision is that the state has a right to imprison Miss Crouse under the doctrine of *parens patriae*. This case encourages other state officials to try to imprison juveniles for noncriminal acts on the basis that such activity is done in the best interests of the child and the state.

1870   *O'Connell v. Turner*. In this case, the parents of a child confined to an institution complain to the courts about the unfair confinement of their child. The case involves a youth named Daniel O'Connell, who is sent to the Chicago Reform School for vagrancy under a law that allows the arrest and trial of people for "misfortune." O'Connell's parents challenge the decision because their child has committed no crime. This time, the Illinois Supreme Court sides with the parents of the institutionalized child saying, in essence, that the state has no right to imprison children for noncriminal acts or for acts that are not clearly specified in the statutes. This decision spawns the "child-saving movement," or at least organized efforts to change state laws. The result of this concerted activity is the ultimate passage of the first delinquency legislation, in Chicago, in 1899. Interestingly, misfortune laws are eventually repealed and the Chicago Reform School is closed in 1872 as a result of the decision reached in the *O'Connell* case.

1905   *Commonwealth v. Fisher.* This is another case coming out of Pennsylvania. The significance of this decision is that the Pennsylvania Supreme Court affirms the legitimacy of juvenile court laws and the right of the state to place a juvenile into an institution—in this case, a house of refuge—until the age of twenty-one or, by extension, the age of majority.

1966   *Kent v. United States.* The case that sets the modern trend for granting juveniles basic rights in the juvenile justice system involves a sixteen-year-old boy, Morris Kent, who is accused of robbery and rape. The case is waived to the adult circuit court without a written reason and without the advice of a lawyer. Subsequently, Kent is found guilty of robbery and housebreaking. The U.S. Supreme Court rules in favor of Kent's appeal and establishes certain minimum requirements in waiver cases, including the right to an attorney during the transfer proceedings. Since the case originates in Washington, D.C., the Court's decision affects only federal jurisdictions

1966   *Miranda v. Arizona.* This is perhaps the most famous U.S. Supreme Court case in the second half of the twentieth century. It ensures that all criminal defendants are given the right to an attorney, or at least receive notification of the right to an attorney, at the point of arrest. The Court's ruling also includes juveniles, but there is some uncertainty about whether the right to an attorney exists for those charged with status offenses.

1967   *In re Gault.* This is the most far–reaching U.S. Supreme Court decision with respect to the rights of juveniles. In

1967,
cont.
this case, Gerald Gault, a fifteen-year-old youth, is charged with making an obscene phone call to a neighbor. The neighbor complains and Gault is arrested, taken to the police station for questioning, and placed into a detention home, all without the knowledge of his parents and without legal counsel. Gault is later found delinquent in juvenile court and is sent to the Arizona Industrial School for an indefinite period, or until he reaches the age of twenty-one. Upon appeal, the Court sides with Gault and sets the stage for the protection of the rights of juveniles in juvenile court. In particular, the decision grants juveniles the right to a lawyer in juvenile court if they are charged with an offense that carries a possible sentence of confinement in a state institution.

1970
In re Winship. In this case, the U.S. Supreme Court decides in favor of a twelve-year-old boy from New York who is charged with larceny and found delinquent based upon a preponderance of evidence. Lawyers for the boy argue that the rules of evidence for deciding criminal charges in juvenile court should use the same standards that apply in adult criminal courts—that is, only evidence that establishes guilt beyond a reasonable doubt can warrant conviction. The Court agrees.

1971
McKeiver v. Pennsylvania. A sixteen-year-old boy, Joseph McKeiver, is charged with robbery and several other felonies and adjudicated in a juvenile court. His request for a jury trial is denied. He is later found delinquent by the juvenile court judge and appeals the decision on the basis of the denial of his request. The U.S. Supreme Court decides in favor of the juvenile court judge's decision, ruling in essence that juveniles do not have a constitutional right to a jury trial in juvenile court. However, the Court does rule that states and communities may allow jury trials in juvenile court if they so desire.

1975
Breed v. Jones. In another case involving the issue of waiver to adult court, the U.S. Supreme Court rules that a juvenile defendant, in this case Jones, cannot be tried in both juvenile and adult courts for the same offense.

Jones is found delinquent of a felony in a California juvenile court and is waived to an adult court, where he is tried and found guilty of the same offense, thus becoming a victim of double jeopardy. It is still possible, of course, for a juvenile court judge or a prosecutor to waive a juvenile case to the adult court system, given certain qualifying conditions. What is not permissible, based upon this ruling, is the actual trial or adjudication of the same case in both court systems.

1984   *Schall v. Martin.* In this case, the U.S. Supreme Court backed away from granting due process protections for juveniles. Martin, a juvenile, is arrested in New York City for robbery, assault, and possessing an illegal weapon. He is subsequently denied freedom and is placed in a detention center. Later, Martin is found delinquent in a juvenile court adjudication hearing. The Supreme Court rules that Martin's conviction is legally valid and that the denial of his request for bail is acceptable under the provisions of the Fifth and Fourteenth amendments to the U.S. Constitution. In essence, the Court rules that juveniles do not have a guarantee to freedom before a trial or adjudication hearing and can be detained for "preventive detention" reasons.

1985   *New Jersey v. T.L.O.* T.L.O. is a New Jersey high school student who is caught smoking in the girls' bathroom at her school. The assistant principal of the school examines her purse against her will and finds evidence of marijuana use and drug dealing. Subsequently, T.L.O. confesses to dealing and is found delinquent in a juvenile court. Her attorneys argue that the evidence obtained in the school search should not have been allowed in court, and the case goes to the U.S. Supreme Court. The Court rules against T.L.O. and thus establishes that evidence seized at school can be obtained without a search warrant and can be used against students in criminal or delinquent cases as long as school officials have a reason to believe that students' property contains evidence or information connected with criminal activity or school policy.

1988   *Thompson v. Oklahoma.* In this case, the U.S. Supreme
        Court establishes that juveniles cannot be executed for
        crimes committed under the age of sixteen. This decision
        is reinforced by subsequent rulings in 1989, in *Wilkins v.
        Missouri* and *Stanford v. Kentucky.* Since the age of sixteen
        appears to be arbitrary to some, it is expected that the
        Court will be asked to review this decision and will pos-
        sibly rule to lower the age limit in the future.

1995   *United States v. Lopez.* The U.S. Supreme Court rules in
        this case that students cannot be charged with unlawful
        gun possession in school under the 1990 federal Gun-
        Free School Zones Act. The case comes out of Texas,
        where a senior high school student is arrested and
        charged with a crime under this federal law. The Court
        rules that the law tries to regulate interstate commerce
        on school grounds and that, in this case, no such com-
        merce has been established. However, the Court allows
        states to pass gun laws banning possession on school
        grounds that do not involve interstate commerce.

2002   *Board of Education of Independent School District No. 92 of
        Pottawatomie County et al. v. Earls et al.* This is the most
        recent U.S. Supreme Court case in which a decision af-
        fecting the rights of juveniles is at issue. In this case, the
        Court rules that school districts may require middle and
        high school students who participate in *any* kind of ex-
        tracurricular activity to submit to drug tests. Essentially,
        the Court rules that the students' right to privacy is off-
        set by the school's right to know who may be using
        drugs in situations that involve school-related activities.
        In part, the privacy rights of students are protected by
        this decision because the results of such testing are not
        to be distributed to those in the authority structure of
        the school system unless there is a demonstrated "need
        to know." Nor are such tests results automatically dis-
        tributed to law enforcement personnel. Any student
        who tests positive for drugs would be refused permis-
        sion to participate in extracurricular activities.

2005   *Roper v. Simmons.* The U.S. Supreme Court considers the
        constitutionality of the death penalty for juveniles. One

important issue is the extent to which juveniles can comprehend the consequences of their actions even in cases of murder or forcible rape. On March 1, 2005 the U.S. Supreme Court bans the use of the death penalty for juveniles under the age of eighteen at the time the crime is committed.

Table 3.1
Overview of Significant Events and Legal Cases, by Time Period

Time Period 1800–1850

Event or Case
New York House of Refuge developed
Probation informally introduced in Boston by John Augustus
Ex Parte Crouse

1850–1900

Children's Aid Society established
First public reformatory, Lyman School for Boys, opened in Massachusetts
Cottage system for juvenile institutions introduced
First probation law passes, in Massachusetts
Hull-House organized
First juvenile court act passed, in Chicago
O'Connell v. Turner

1900–1950

Commonwealth v. Fisher
Child-guidance clinics established
U.S. Children's Bureau formed

1950–present

Kent v. United States
Miranda v. Arizona
In re Gault
Challenge of Crime in a Free Society published, creating Law Enforcement Assistance Administration and criminal justice program grants
Juvenile Justice and Delinquency Prevention Act passed, in part creating the Office of Juvenile Justice and Delinquency Prevention
McKeiver v. Pennsylvania
Breed v. Jones
Schall v. Martin
New Jersey v. T.L.O.
Boot camps and restorative justice used as prevention programs for juvenile offenders
Board of Education of Independent School District No. 92 of Pottawatomie County et al. v. Earls et al.
In *Roper v. Simmons*, U.S. Supreme Court overrules the constitutionality of the death penalty for juveniles

References

Addams, Jane. 1910. *Twenty Years at Hull-House.* New York: Macmillan.

Empey, Lamar T., Mark C. Stafford, and Carter H. Hay. 1999. *American Delinquency: Its Meaning and Construction,* 4th ed. Boston: Wadsworth.

Grossberg, Michael. 2002. "Changing Conceptions of Child Welfare in the United States, 1820–1935." Pp. 3–41 in Margaret K. Rosenheim, Franklin E. Zimring, David S. Tanenhaus, and Bernardine Dohrn, eds., *A Century of Juvenile Justice.* Chicago: University of Chicago Press.

Mennel, Robert M. 1973. *Thorns & Thistles: Juvenile Delinquents in the United States, 1825–1940.* Hanover, NH: University Press of New England.

Parry, David L., ed. 2005. *Essential Readings in Juvenile Justice.* Upper Saddle River, NJ: Pearman/Prentice-Hall.

Platt, Anthony M. 1977. *Child Savers: The Invention of Delinquency,* 2nd ed., enlarged. Chicago: University of Chicago Press.

Rothman, David J. 1971. *Discovery of the Asylum: Social Order and Disorder in the New Republic.* Boston: Little, Brown.

Siegel, Larry J., and Joseph J. Senna. 2000. *Juvenile Delinquency: Theory, Practice, and Law,* 7th ed. Belmont, CA: Wadsworth.

Web Sources

www.ncianet.org

http://chicagoareaproject.org/hist_pioneers.htm

www.Britannica.com/women/articles/Lathrop_Julia_Clifford.html

www.spartacus.schoolnet.co.uk/USAWbowen.htm

These are excellent sources of information concerning the history and mission of Hull-House in Chicago, as well as biographical information on its leaders, such as Jane Addams and Louise Bowen.

4

People and Events

The first three chapters of this book identify significant historical and contemporary characteristics of the juvenile justice system in the United States. We have discussed problems and controversies within this system and have suggested some solutions. We have also described the efforts of individuals and organizations that helped develop the system of handling youthful offenders. In this chapter, we will take a closer look at several people and events that have had an impact on the U.S. juvenile justice system. These topics and biographical descriptions will be presented in alphabetical order.

Jane Addams (1860–1935)

One of the most prominent child-saving institutions was Chicago's Hull-House, which Jane Addams founded in 1889 and led during the late nineteenth and early twentieth centuries. Hull-House was a settlement house, one of the first of its kind in Chicago. This institution provided many services to the city's residents, most of which were aimed at the disadvantaged, the poor, and the immigrant. For example, Hull-House was the first such facility in Chicago to establish citizenship classes, a public playground, a gymnasium, and a public swimming pool. Hull-House was also the first organization in the city to conduct investigations of truancy, test reading skills of children, and establish a Boy Scout troop. The institution was also instrumental in establishing factory laws to protect child workers. One of the residents of Hull-House, Alzina Stevens, was the first probation officer in the city.

As its founder, Jane Addams was the most prominent leader of Hull-House. She became an active leader of the child-saving movement, first through Hull-House activities, then later through national and international activities. Addams was also instrumental in establishing research centers addressing the needs of youth, such as the Juvenile Protective Association and, perhaps most important of all, the first juvenile court in the world in 1899.

In 1910 Addams wrote *Twenty Years at Hull-House,* in which she outlined many of her philosophical ideas concerning social justice and the role of voluntary associations and organizations in promoting human rights and justice, especially for minority youth. In particular, she supported the civic value of social clubs in promoting social responsibility and civic awareness for the club members and for the greater community as well. She was convinced that promoting the welfare of all, including the most disadvantaged in a community, would ultimately promote social advancement for the whole society. She was also a strong Christian and tried to recruit members of Hull-House and supporters of social reform who shared her beliefs about strict sexual morals. Social activities at the settlement house were strictly supervised, especially those for single females. Once Addams refused to admit to Hull-House two teenage girls who had been rescued from a house of prostitution because she felt they would not be accepted by the settlement community.

Later, Addams became president of the National Conference of Charities and Corrections, which became the National Conference of Social Work. Toward the end of her career, Addams turned her interests to political activism, but still with the goal of social reform. She became more interested in women's rights and peacemaking efforts and was the first president of the Women's International League for Peace and Freedom. In 1931 she received the Nobel Peace Prize.

Freda Adler (1934–)

In 1975, Freda Adler's book *Sisters in Crime: The Rise of the New Female Criminal* was published. Adler's book examined arrest data from 1960 to 1972 from the FBI's *Uniform Crime Reports.* Adler noticed that the percentages for female arrest rates during this period had dramatically increased and concluded that the increase was a direct result of the women's movement and women gaining more freedom. Adler predicted that female crime and delinquency rates would continue to increase as women integrated into the workforce and became more like men. This phenomenon is known as the emancipation theory. Today, female crime and delinquency rates remain relatively low in comparison to those rates for males. Female incarceration rates have risen, but this has occurred because the war on drugs has resulted in more women than ever before entering the criminal justice system on drug-related offenses. Adler's methods and theory have been criticized, but her book helped change the way that women and girls are viewed in criminology. Before this book, theories of female criminality and delinquency were based on females being inferior biologically to males, and environmental and sociological factors were not even considered. Adler was the first to address female criminality and delinquency from a sociological rather than biological perspective.

John Augustus (1785–1859)

John Augustus was the first individual to actually work with convicted offenders in the capacity of what today we would call probation. Probation allows a convicted criminal to remain out of prison or jail to serve his or her sentence under the supervision of a probation officer. The practice can be traced to the 1820s, in England, but most scholars agree that Augustus was the first to use probation as we know it today. Augustus was a Boston shoemaker who vouched for those who had been convicted of crimes in Boston courts. Although he had no formal education or specific training for working with criminals, Augustus would take over the rehabilitation of these convicts for a period of one year or more. Afterward, he would take the criminals back to court to prove to a judge that they had reformed and that imprisonment was unnecessary. The concept of probation became an official policy of Massachusetts law in 1869. By the end of the nineteenth century, probation for juvenile offenders had become a permanent part of the state's juvenile justice system.

Augustus originally worked with adults, but early in his career, he became a defender of juveniles and began to take on more and more juvenile cases. He once wrote, "In 1846, I became bail to the amount of $3,000, in the Police Court . . . . That year I became surety for eleven boys, who were arrested for larceny;

they were young, being from nine to thirteen years old" (cited in Mennel 1973, 43).

Today, probation is considered a workhorse of the U.S. juvenile justice system. Probation exists in virtually every juvenile court jurisdiction and is used for over half of all youth convicted of crimes or status offenses (Bartollas 2003, 446). Because of his efforts and the unceasing interest he showed in developing the potential for living a law-abiding life among convicted criminals, young and old, many people today refer to Augustus as the "father of probation."

Howard Becker (1928–)

Howard Becker was born in Chicago and lived in an area characterized by racial and ethnic diversity. Early in his life, he was influenced by music, especially the piano, and he became a professional piano player as a young man. He attended graduate school at the University of Chicago at an early age and eventually found research resources on the topics of personality, social psychology, and occupations, especially medical occupations.

In the early 1950s, Becker began to develop his ideas on social interaction and social organizations, ideas that later became associated with the labeling perspective and its attendant treatment and correctional policies, including diversion (see Chapter 2). A major work in this field was Becker's book *Outsiders: Studies in the Sociology of Deviance*, which was published in 1963. In this book, and in many other writings from the 1960s and 1970s, Becker enunciated the major ideas and concepts of labeling theory, including the idea that people form self-identities through organizational and group memberships, and that labeling people as criminals can create changes in their self-perceptions. It is this emphasis on the reactions of society to the behavior of its members that clearly casts Becker's ideas into the field of labeling theory.

Although Becker has not published much in this field in the past several years, he remains an influential figure in the area of self-perception and the effects of labeling people as deviant on their self-concepts and behavior patterns.

Louise Bowen (1859–1953)

Louise Bowen was an important contributor to the financial and policy-making efforts of Hull-House. Her contemporary, Jane

Addams, estimated that she contributed over $750,000 to Hull-House. However, Bowen was also a strong advocate of human rights and social welfare, and in that respect, she was a loyal follower of Jane Addams. Bowen was a strong Christian, as was Addams, and seemed to prefer living with minority and disadvantaged people, especially youth. She also spent money for the establishment of a rural settlement house, similar to Hull-House, for poor children from Chicago.

Bowen was also involved in studies of youth and African Americans in Chicago and led many of the programs run by Hull-House to improve the lives of disadvantaged people, including minority youth. The book *The Colored People of Chicago,* published in 1913, was one product of these interests and activities. Bowen also led many drives to rid Chicago of vice areas, which she felt were contributing to the moral decay and destructive behaviors of youth. As president of the Juvenile Protective Association, founded in 1907, she was able to develop and implement many of these youth-oriented projects.

Although she was associated with the Republican Party, Bowen did not translate her social zeal and willingness to spend money on the plight of the poor and disadvantaged into politics. In that respect, she was different from Addams. Bowen chose instead to stay out of political issues and the support of political personalities and to concentrate on social and financial programs for poor and minority children and the plight of specific children who were in need.

Both Addams and Bowen have been characterized as strong-willed women who approached juvenile justice reform with a strong passion and resolve. Anthony Platt observed, "Louise Bowen acted on her conscience and, once convinced that a wrong needed righting, attacked the problem with all of her resources and energy" (Platt 1977, 87). They both had a genuine concern for poor and immigrant families and worked hard to create opportunities for these families to get a chance at a successful life in the United States and for their children to get a good education and a life free of crime and delinquency.

Charles Brace (1826–1890)

Charles Brace founded the Children's Aid Society (CAS) in New York in 1853. He was especially interested in ridding the city of poor and delinquent children. One of the purposes of this organization was to provide family housing arrangements for poor and delinquent youth who might otherwise be placed in institutions. Based largely on the assumption that the evil characteristics of the city led many youth astray, Brace and his colleagues often arranged for children to be placed in homes located in rural areas and often in states far away from New York, such as Florida, Texas, California, Iowa, Michigan, and Missouri, to name a few. This practice became known as "placing out" or "farming out." The idea was to place troubled youth, not necessarily criminal offenders, in homes and with families that were considered stable and healthy. The traditional family, particularly in a rural setting, with a working father and a mother who was able to care for children was considered an ideal placement. The program was an important element of nineteenth-century juvenile corrections policies; as many as an estimated 92,000 youngsters were sent to families outside of New York during that century. Brace once said, "The beginning of a farmer, my boys, is the making of a Congressman, and a President" (Mennel 1973, 38).

In contrast to Jane Addams and Louise Bowen, some have suggested that Brace had little sympathy for poor and immigrant youth. He thought of them as street children who were in need of kind and gentle, or not-so-gentle in some cases, correction. Brace once said, "Whatever . . . sympathy we may have with the poorest subjects put under our care, I hold that it is impossible for a man to feel towards them in any degree as a father feels towards his own offspring" (cited in Mennel 1973, 47). Brace felt these juvenile offenders were dangerous to others and to society as a whole. He even suggested that young delinquents would become a significant menace to the welfare of democracy and civil order if they were allowed to grow up without any correction or intervention in their lives. As he put it, "Let but law lift its hand from them for a season, or let the civilizing influences of American life fail to reach them, . . . and, if opportunity offered, we should see an explosion from this class which might leave this city in ashes and blood" (cited in Binder, Geis, and Bruce 1997, 206).

Regardless of how Brace and his colleagues really viewed the youth placed in their care and supervision, some scholars believe that the CAS was the first organization to establish a foster home system for neglected and wayward youth. Moreover, there is ample evidence that the efforts of the CAS often resulted in positive reforms for children placed out under its supervision. Some of the children in the program became successful farmers, lawyers, doctors, ministers, and even governors of states and U.S. territories. While the CAS and similar programs had many supporters and positive outcomes of its placing-out policies, there were many negative issues surrounding the organization and its policies. Not the least of these was that Brace and his colleagues focused on poor and immigrant youth to the exclusion of others and seemed to cater to the welfare of the foster families as much as they did to the rehabilitation of the children themselves, if not more so.

Zebulon Brockway (1827–1920)

Zebulon Brockway was born into a successful family in Connecticut and grew up with economic comfort. However, rather than choosing a life in the world of business, Brockway decided to devote his life to social improvements, particularly prison reform. He worked his way up the hierarchy of prison management, starting at the bottom in Rochester, New York, and advancing through the ranks to become the superintendent of the Detroit House of Correction for eleven years before becoming the administrator of the newly established Elmira Reformatory in 1876 (see Chapter 1). He remained in that position for almost a quarter of a century.

At an early age, Brockway became convinced that prisons were little more than concrete and mortar fortresses and warehouses for prisoners. He saw little opportunity within prison walls for rehabilitation or human reform. Later in his career, he was instrumental in forming the National Prison Congress in 1870, held in Cincinnati, and for disseminating its "Declaration of Principles" to prison reformers, educators, and the public throughout most of the rest of that century. Although his career involved the supervision of adult prisoners, his reformist philosophies and his work at the Elmira Reformatory influenced institutional changes for juveniles.

Through Brockway's pursuit of introducing indeterminate sentencing, he became a leader of prison reform for adults and juveniles. His efforts and philosophies demonstrated the value of open sentencing for rehabilitation and personal change among inmates. But he also advocated using the "scientific" approach to understanding human behavior and its control rather than "sickly sentimentalism" (Platt 1977, 47). Despite his emphasis on treatment, rehabilitation, and indeterminate sentences, Brockway used strict discipline, patterned after the military, and hard work as a regular part of the Elmira system. For example, he was not reluctant to use whipping and other means of corporal punishment to control recalcitrant inmates. Toward the end of his career, in 1912, Brockway published an influential autobiography, *Fifty Years of Prison Service.*

Meda Chesney-Lind (1947–)

Chesney-Lind is a self-identified feminist scholar who studies the impact of the criminal and juvenile justice systems on female offenders and defendants. As such, she has noted that the criminal justice system and the majority of theories on crime are based on male criminal behavior. These theories are then applied to female delinquency and crime without taking into consideration gender differences. Girls who are status offenders, for example, are often in detention for running away from home; frequently the reason is to escape physical, sexual, or emotional abuse. Their prior victimization is often not addressed while in detention because the juvenile justice system was created for boys, who are rarely in detention for status offenses. Chesney-Lind has helped bring attention to the needs of girls and women who are offenders and has helped make policy makers aware of the differences between male and female offenders to provide better treatment and services. Chesney-Lind has received many research and service awards from professional societies; the University of Hawaii at Manoa, where she works; and from the state of Hawaii for her scholarly work as well as for her activities in civic affairs. One of her most recent works is the second edition of *The Female Offender,* co-authored with Lisa Pasko (2004).

Sigmund Freud (1856–1939)

Perhaps the best known psychiatrist of the late nineteenth and early twentieth centuries was Sigmund Freud. Freud is well known for developing the psychoanalytic view of human behavior. While Freud did not have a great deal to say about crime and delinquency specifically, many of his student and followers, such as August Aichhorn, used his ideas to develop elaborate theoretical explanations and treatment programs based on these explanations. Psychoanalytic theory assumes that people grow and develop in stages of sexual maturity and that during any of these stages, problems can occur that can affect one's personality and behavior later in life. According to this theory, most problems that develop in adolescence or adulthood have causes that begin early in life. Furthermore, the individual develops defense mechanisms that mask or hide the real source of the problem and conceal their true origin. Consequently, time-consuming and expensive projective techniques must be used by the therapist to help the patient confront the underlying issues causing his or her behavior. These techniques include dream analysis, hypnosis, and projective tests such as the Rorschach test. Within the field of juvenile justice, psychoanalytic techniques are still used in individual counseling and therapeutic programs. Because of the time and cost that psychoanalytic therapies usually entail, however, many psychological counseling programs have moved away from psychoanalysis and toward more objective and direct methods of therapy (see Chapter 1).

Lawrence Kohlberg (1927–)

Lawrence Kohlberg popularized the concept of moral development. Kohlberg and his associates theorized that people develop in stages of moral responsibility and personal conscience. As young children, we are guided by what Kohlberg calls the "preconventional" stage of reasoning. In this level, children are influenced by the threat of punishment from parents or guardians if they fail to abide by established rules. Teenagers usually mature beyond the pre-conventional stage and operate according to the "conventional" stage of moral reasoning, obeying laws and rules because of a belief in their validity. As adults, we normally progress to a "post-conventional" stage of reasoning, whereby we are guided by our own personal consciousness and internal acceptance of society's rules. At this stage, one's personal beliefs and set of ethics can sometimes overrule societal laws, especially if these internal guides are based upon what one considers to be universal principles (Adler, Mueller, and Laufer 2002).

According to Kohlberg, delinquents usually operate at the level of pre-conventional reasoning, which means that their treatment should be based on efforts to improve the way they consider the consequences of their actions and the reasons for obeying laws and rules of society. When applied to the treatment of inmates, adult and juvenile, this theoretical approach has shown some positive results but, as with virtually all theories and treatment programs, not all delinquents and criminals benefit from this approach to rehabilitation.

Julia Clifford Lathrop (1858–1932)

Julia Lathrop was an influential leader in the development of the first juvenile delinquency law in Chicago. Lathrop was born in Rockford, Illinois, and was a member of the philanthropic and educated segment of Illinois society. She received a degree from Vassar College in 1880 and worked for her father for many years. She became active in social and political reform for juveniles; in particular, her interests were in social work and the social welfare of children. Along with her close friend and associate Lucy Flower, Lathrop became a major figure in the passage of the nation's first juvenile delinquency law in Chicago. She was also active in Hull-House and the first female member of the influential Illinois State Board of Charities. In 1912, President William Howard Taft appointed her to the board of the U.S. Children's Bureau. Lathrop remained active in political and social reform, including women's suffrage, until her death in her hometown of Rockford in 1932 (Tanenhaus 2002; Platt 1977).

Benjamin Barr Lindsey (1896–1943)

Benjamin Barr Lindsey was the first full-time juvenile court judge, serving as an elected judge for the Denver, Colorado, juvenile court from 1900 to 1927. Although the first juvenile court of law was established in Chicago, Lindsey is known as the first judge to work only with juvenile cases, certainly in the United States if not in the world. He became aware of the conditions of poor children in the justice system when he became legal counsel to street youth, many of whom were staying in "wine rooms" and local brothels, in addition to being housed with adult criminals in the Denver jail (Rodgers 1993).

Lindsey was born in Jackson, Tennessee, to parents who came from wealthy families in Mississippi. He moved with his family to Denver when he was a teenager, but there the family did not fare well financially. Perhaps that is one reason why he was socially concerned and aware of the plight of the poor, especially poor children (Lindsey 1909). He was politically and socially active for all of his judicial years in Colorado. This activity undoubtedly put him at odds with many conservative and powerful people, including the leaders of the Ku Klux Klan, which was emerging at that time in Denver. Despite his declining popularity in Colorado, Lindsey is credited with improving the lives of many young people and with outlining the essential philosophy of the traditional juvenile justice system in the United States and around the world.

Cesare Lombroso (1835–1909)

Cesare Lombroso was the leader of what is known as the "Positive School" in the field of criminology. Lombroso was an Italian physician who was often called upon to perform autopsies on the cadavers of infamous criminals. Through his work, Lombroso eventually came upon the idea that criminals were genetically predisposed (that is, criminals were born with a genetic or biological tendency to commit crime) and that a person's preordained future could be determined by physical appearance. According to Lombroso, criminals looked different from other people. Their physical features included cauliflower-shaped ears, solitary lines in the palm, low foreheads, and even tattoos. At first, he believed that all criminals had been born with the tendency to commit crime and that criminals were atavistic, or representative of evolutionary throwbacks. Later in his career, Lombroso altered his views, concluding that only around 40 percent of criminals were atavists.

While Lombroso did not advocate the death penalty as a proper societal response to crime, his ideas did promote what has become known as eugenics; that is, the involuntary sterilization of criminals and mentally retarded people in order to improve the genetic pool. Eugenics laws were passed in many states during the twentieth century, and surgical sterilizations were often practiced on youth committed to reformatories and other institutions.

Robert Merton (1910–2003)

Robert Merton was probably the best known sociologist of the twentieth century. His works and ideas influenced several subfields of sociology, including crime and delinquency. Merton was born into modest circumstances in a poor section of Philadelphia and, as a gang member, learned from an early age the value of physical prowess and the ability to develop street smarts.

Despite these inauspicious beginnings, Merton excelled in school and eventually enrolled in graduate studies at Harvard University. There, he was deftly able to combine his street smarts with his intellectual acumen and began a career that spanned many decades and influenced thousands of young scholars and practitioners, especially in the area of social programs for the treatment and rehabilitation of juvenile and adult offenders.

Although Merton was a prolific scholar, he is perhaps best known for his theory of anomie and crime (*Social Theory and Social Structure* 1957). This theory argues that people in lower- and working-class positions strive for monetary success but are unable to compete successfully through established, legitimate channels, particularly education. Consequently, they are often influenced to strive for success through illegitimate means, including criminal and delinquent behavior. This important idea has been the theoretical basis, albeit with numerous modifications, of many crime and delinquency prevention programs, including Head Start. Such programs are based on the notion that providing youngsters with resources and encouragement for educational and economic success will eventually reduce their attraction to criminal means for achieving success. In many ways, these programs have been successful (Adler, Mueller, and Laufer 2002).

Jerome G. Miller (1931–)

Jerome Miller is best known for his efforts to reform the juvenile correctional system in Massachusettts (see Chapter 2). After working with the Massachusetts Department of Youth Services in the early 1970s, Miller worked with the Illinois Department of Youth and Family Services and the Pennsylvania Commission of Children and Youth. In both states, he attempted juvenile correctional reform, but not to the same extent that he had done in Massachusetts. Miller's book *Last One over the Wall* (1991) details the closing of juvenile institutions in Massachusetts. In 1996, he published another book, *Search & Destroy: African Americans in the Criminal Justice System,* which provides discussions of race and punishment in U.S. society. After several years of leading juvenile justice reform in Massachusetts, Illinois, and Pennsylvania, Miller is now co-founder and president of the National Center on Institutions and Alternatives, a nonprofit organization based in Alexandria, Virginia (http://www.ncianet.org).

Clifford Shaw (1896–1957)

Clifford Shaw was born in Luray, Indiana, and grew up in a family of ten children. His family was middle class, and life in rural Indiana near the turn of the twentieth century was close knit and comfortable for the young criminologist. At an early age, Shaw recognized the importance of informality and consideration in the treatment of juvenile offenders when a blacksmith showed him just that kind of attitude when he was caught stealing from the tradesman. In the 1920s, while a student at the University of Chicago, Shaw became a parole officer for the state of Illinois and eventually found work in the juvenile court system in Chicago, which passed the country's first juvenile delinquency law in 1899.

After his work in the juvenile court system, Shaw became interested in research on youth and society and eventually developed a significant research program at the University of Chicago. During this time, he teamed with a former graduate student colleague, Henry McKay, to conduct a series of studies on delinquency and area of residence in Chicago, which later developed into studies in other cities. From these studies, his years as a parole officer, and his earlier experiences as a youth in rural Indiana, Shaw, along with McKay, developed what has become known as the theory of social disorganization, an important contribution to the study of juvenile delinquency for over fifty years (Shaw et al. 1929; Shaw and McKay 1942). This theory assumes that delinquency is attributable more to where people live than to their individual characteristics. In the early 1930s, Shaw developed a delinquency prevention project known as the Chicago Area Project (CAP). The CAP tries to reduce delinquency by encouraging lay leaders, such as teachers, school administrators, business leaders, and church leaders, to work with youth in their neighborhoods and to provide wholesome recreational opportunities for these young people. By the early 1990s the CAP had spread into other cities in Illinois (*V.I.P. Examiner* 1992).

Society for the Prevention of Cruelty to Children

The Society for the Prevention of Cruelty to Children (SPCC) was created in New York in 1874. Within thirty years, there were over 300 chapters throughout the Untied States. This organization tried to help troubled juveniles to change their lives and become productive adults. We do not know how successful these efforts were, but it was common in those days for such agencies to be directly involved in the rehabilitation of many urban youth, especially those youngsters from poor, immigrant, and lower-class backgrounds living in inner-city and slum areas. The SPCC also helped create laws and policies that protected youth from abusive parents and neglectful situations.

Edwin H. Sutherland (1853–1950)

Edwin H. Sutherland was one of the most prolific scholars of criminology in the twentieth century. He is known for having coined the term *white-collar crime* and for developing the theory of differential association, one of the most influential theoretical explanations of crime and delinquency. This theory has nine major propositions, but essentially it maintains that people learn patterns of criminal behavior in much the same way that they learn to do anything else. Crime and delinquency are learned by associating with people who display patterns of criminal behavior, including attitudes and techniques for committing crime. For juveniles, these associations are particularly evident in close, personal groups such as the family and peer groups. This theory supports different kinds of group therapy techniques, such as guided-group interaction and positive peer culture, which are used in correctional settings, such as institutions and halfway homes. Such therapies are based on the idea that behavior is learned, especially in social settings, and that social settings for delinquents can be altered to produce conventional attitudes and behaviors. If peers can be used to turn people around, and if the individual can also be used to help turn around others, then rehabilitation can be more easily accomplished.

Enoch C. Wines (1806–1879)

Another important contributor to the child-saving movement in the nineteenth century was Enoch C. Wines. According to Anthony Platt, author of a historical account of the lives, activities, and contributions of the child savers, Enoch Wines was "the foremost American authority on reformatories and institutions for children prior to the twentieth century" (Platt 1977, 48). Wines was a champion for prisoner care and fair treatment of inmates in prisons or correctional institutions. In 1871, as the leader of the New York Commission on Prison Labor, he exposed many instances of inhumane conditions for juveniles in the New York House of Refuge, especially in the area of labor within the institution. Over his career, Wines published several accounts of prison and reformatory life and the conditions of these institutions. Chief among these was the 1867 *Report on the Prisons and Reformatories of the United States and Canada,* co-authored with Theodore Dwight. In this report, Wines and Dwight concluded that inmate reform had been lost in the philosophies of prison administrators and that such goals should be made essential in future prison programs, including reformatories. As they put it, "What we want . . . is to gain the will, the consent, the cooperation of these men, not to mould them into so many pieces of machinery" (cited in Rothman 1971, 244).

In place of prisons, Wines advocated the creation of more reformatories, which he saw as the hope of the future for correctional institutions, especially for juveniles. According to Wines, reformatories would be able to counteract the negative influences of bad families and poor social environments, unlike any other correctional program or institution. However, these institutions should be established to rehabilitate and reform the inmate, not simply warehouse. To place his ideas into practice, Wines was also instrumental in the establishment of the Elmira Reformatory, which was founded in 1869 and officially opened in 1877. In Chapter 1, we discussed the operations and philosophy of that institution, and its first administrator, Zebulon Brockway. After his death in 1879, Enoch Wines's son, Frederick Wines, edited his last book, *The State of Prisons and of Child-Saving Institutions in the Civilized World,* and published it in 1880. Frederick Wines later became one of the leaders in prison reform in the latter part of the nineteenth century.

References

Addams, Jane. 1910. *Twenty Years at Hull-House.* New York: Macmillan.

Adler, Freda. 1975. *Sisters in Crime: The Rise of the New Female Criminal.* New York: McGraw-Hill.

Adler, Freda, Gerhard O. W. Mueller, and William S. Laufer. 2002. *Criminology and the Criminal Justice System,* 4th ed. New York: McGraw-Hill.

Barnes, Harry Elmer, and Negley Teeters. 1959. *New Horizons in Criminology,* 3rd ed. Englewood Cliffs, NJ: Prentice-Hall.

Bartollas, Clemens. 2003. *Juvenile Delinquency,* 6th ed. New York: Allyn and Bacon.

Binder, Arnold, Gilbert Geis, and Dickson D. Bruce, Jr. 1997. *Juvenile Delinquency: Historical, Cultural, and Legal Perspectives,* 2nd ed. Cincinnati, OH: Anderson.

Chesney-Lind, Meda. 1997. *The Female Offender: Girls, Women and Crime.* Thousand Oaks, CA: Sage.

Chesney-Lind, Meda, and Lisa Pasko. 2004. *The Female Offender: Girls, Women, and Crime,* 2nd ed. Thousand Oaks, CA: Sage.

Drowns, Robert W., and Karen M. Hess. 1992. *Juvenile Justice,* 2nd ed. New York: West.

Lindsey, Judge Ben B. 1909. "The Beast and the Jungle." *Everybody's Magazine* (October): 433–452.

Martin, Randy, Robert J. Mutchnick, and W. Timothy Austin. 1990. *Criminological Thought: Pioneers Past and Present.* New York: Macmillan.

Mays, G. Larry, and L. Thomas Winfree, Jr. 1999. *Juvenile Justice.* New York: McGraw-Hill.

Mennel, Robert M. 1973. *Thorns & Thistles: Juvenile Delinquents in the United States, 1825–1940.* Hanover, NH: University Press of New England.

Merton, Robert K. 1957. *Social Theory and Social Structure,* revised and enlarged edition. New York: Free Press.

Miller, Jerome G. 1991. *Last One over the Wall: The Massachusetts Experiment in Closing Reform Schools.* Columbus, OH: Ohio State University Press.

———. 1996. *Search and Destrroy: African-American Males in the Criminal Justice System.* Cambridge: Cambridge University Press.

Platt, Anthony M. 1977. *The Child Savers: The Invention of Delinquency,* 2nd ed., enlarged. Chicago: University of Chicago Press.

Rodgers, Frederick B. 1992. "Benjamin Barr Lindsey." *The Colorado Lawyer* (July): 1427–1429.

Rothman, David J. 1971. *The Discovery of the Asylum: Social Order and Disorder in the New Republic.* Boston: Little, Brown.

Shaw, Clifford R., and Henry D. McKay. 1942. *Juvenile Delinquency and Urban Areas.* Chicago: University of Chicago Press.

Shaw, Clifford R., Frederick M. Zorbaugh, Henry D. McKay, and Leonard D. Cottrell. 1929. *Delinquency Areas.* Chicago: University of Chicago Press.

Siegel, Larry J. 2002. *Juvenile Delinquency: The Core.* Belmont, CA: Wadsworth/Thompson Learning.

Siegel, Larry J., and Joseph J. Senna. 2000. *Juvenile Delinquency: Theory, Practice, and Law,* 7th ed. Belmont, CA: Wadsworth.

Sullivan, Dennis, and Larry Tifft. 1996. *Restorative Justice: Healing the Foundations of Our Everyday Lives.* Monsey, NY: Willow Tree.

Tanenhaus, David S. 2002. "The Evolution of Juvenile Courts in the Early Twentieth Century: Beyond the Myth of Immaculate Construction." Pp. 42–73 in Margaret K. Rosenheim, Franklin E. Zimring, David S. Tanenhaus, and Bernardine Dohrn, eds., *A Century of Juvenile Justice.* Chicago: University of Chicago Press.

U.S. Department of Justice. 2000. *Title V Community Prevention Grants Program: 2000 Report to Congress.* Washington, DC: Office of Juvenile Justice and Delinquency Prevention.

V.I.P. Examiner. 1992. "Chicago Area Project: A Delinquency Prevention Model." *V.I.P. Examiner* (Summer): 6–11, 14–17.

Web Sources:

www.Britannica.com/women/articles/Lathrop_Julia_Clifford.html

www.ncianet.org

http://chicagoareaproject.org/history.htm

www.spartacus.schoolnet.co.uk/USAhullhouse.htm

These are excellent sources of information concerning the history and mission of Hull-House in Chicago and its leaders.

5

Facts and Figures

I n this chapter, we present some of the latest research findings regarding juveniles, their involvement in delinquent behavior, their victimization experiences, problems they face (for example, suicide, school failure, and teen pregnancy), and the social reaction to their behavior. More specifically, we present data on basic juvenile population demographics, juveniles as offenders, juvenile court and correctional trends, juveniles as victims, and youth in crisis. We examine, among other things, (1) the size of the U.S. juvenile population; (2) the number of youth who are arrested for serious delinquent acts; (3) the most significant trends in juvenile justice; (4) the factors associated with juvenile crime victimization; and (5) trends in social problems affecting U.S. juveniles.

It is important for us to note that there is so much data on juvenile justice that a review of social science research findings can be overwhelming. In order to help the reader make sense of what can be very confusing (and sometimes contradictory) material, we have endeavored to make this presentation as clear and user friendly as possible. By focusing on the bigger picture of delinquency and juvenile justice, we will try to help the reader understand the major issues, long-term trends, and lasting concerns and criticisms.

No one empirical study, no single measure of delinquency can tell us everything we would like to know. To understand delinquency, juvenile justice, and other problems facing young people, it is much more useful and enlightening to look at the accumulation of research findings, the broader trends, and the historical and cultural background of issues. As we have made clear in earlier chapters, we believe that history and the wider culture shape the present and influence the future. Readers interested in more detailed information should consult Chapters 6 and 7 after completing this chapter, as these two chapters list agencies and organizations, as well as print and nonprint resources, that will help fill in the gaps. We begin our discussion on facts and figures by dispelling a few myths.

Misperceptions and Misunderstandings

More than anything else, we set out in this chapter to correct common misperceptions regarding the nature of delinquency and the juvenile justice system. Chief among these myths is the notion that delinquency is spiraling ever upward. This common, though regrettable, misperception is understandable given the popular media's coverage of sensational cases (for example, the killing spree that took place at Colorado's Columbine High School in 1999). The reality, however, is this: delinquency, particularly the most serious and violent acts (such as robbery and homicide), increased dramatically from the mid-1980s to the early 1990s. Since about 1994, however, there has been a sharp and steady decrease in serious delinquency. We will look closer at this and other trends later in the chapter.

Another popular myth is that the juvenile justice system is soft on delinquency. In fact, as we will show, the criminal justice system generally and the juvenile justice system particularly have become increasingly harsh and punitive (Beckett and Sasson 2004; Miller 1996). This crackdown or "get tough" approach to crime and delinquency has occurred despite the fact that crime and delinquency rates are actually down. Today, we are incarcerating a record number of people—more than 2 million individuals (this includes adults and juveniles)—in our jails, prisons, and juvenile institutions. The number of juveniles who are waived or transferred to the adult criminal justice system is also growing. Boot camps and other such incarceration programs have multiplied in recent years. These policies hardly represent a soft or lenient response to delinquency.

A related myth is that justice in the United States is blind to race, class, and gender. Courthouses across the country contain images of Lady Justice wearing a blindfold and holding the scales of justice in her hands. The ideal is that every accused person is afforded a fair and reasonable chance to rigorously defend himself or herself from the charges filed against them. The reality, however, is that our "get tough" policies have disproportionately affected minorities, especially young African American males (Maurer 1999; Miller 1996). In some places (for example, Baltimore and Washington, D.C.), more than half of all African American males between eighteen and thirty-five are under the control of the criminal justice system. Nationwide, the proportion is closer to one-third of black males between eighteen and twenty-five (Beckett and Sasson 2004). There is now widespread agreement among criminologists and other legal experts that extralegal factors (e.g., race, class, and gender) play an important role in processing juvenile and criminal justice cases. Justice in the United States is not blind. As one author puts it, "the rich get richer and the poor get prison" (Reiman 2004).

Many people might think the reduction in crime and delinquency is directly tied to "get tough" policies and the rapid and massive increase in rates of incarceration. That may seem to be a logical conclusion, but the data do not support this interpretation.

For one thing, crime rates had already been declining when many of these "get tough" policies were implemented. Drug use was clearly dropping before many legislatures stepped up their war on drugs, for example, in the form of mandatory minimum sentences. For another, nonviolent, low-level drug offenders account for most of the record growth in our inmate population (Mauer 1999). Americans may talk about the need to punish violent offenders, but the reality is that we are punishing record numbers of nonviolent offenders. Finally, the available evidence does not support a connection between increasingly punitive policies and a reduction in crime. Crime and delinquency rates are affected by a number of interacting factors. The change in criminal justice policy alone could not have had such an influence on crime and delinquency (Mauer 1999). Ironically, it may be the case that retributive justice or overly punitive policies undermine the well-being of families and communities and thereby contribute to more rather than less crime and delinquency (Beckett and Sasson 2004).

Fortunately, the adult and juvenile justice systems are not as one-dimensional as we have made them out to be. While the overall trend has been toward greater punishment and retribution, a number of other, more helpful policies and programs have been initiated. For example, some communities in the United States and across the world have been following a restorative justice model, an approach that emphasizes a balanced approach to wrongdoing. Offenders are made to accept responsibility for their actions, victims and their needs and concerns are brought into the process, and the community's right to safety and peace is acknowledged and protected. The emphasis with restorative justice is on restoring the situation to one of wholeness, whereas the retributive model of justice emphasizes "just deserts" or revenge.

In addition to restorative justice efforts, delinquency prevention and control programs have improved significantly over the past decades. Today there is convincing evidence that some well-thought-out and carefully designed prevention and treatment programs, such as multisystemic therapy (MST) and drug courts, are successful (Lundman 2001). MST is a relatively new type of intensive counseling that significantly reduces delinquent behavior. Drug courts are special courts of law that focus on the unique problems associated with drug users and dealers. Both MST and drug courts are a welcome alternative to the failed programs (like boot camps and "scared straight" programs) that remain popular with many policy makers.

While there has been some recent success in reducing crime and delinquency, it would be unwise to claim victory over the problem of juvenile crime. Put a bit differently, as a nation we should be proud of the dramatic reduction in serious youth violence that has occurred in recent years, but we would be foolish indeed to let down our guard. If we ignore the problems facing many of our juveniles, it would be at our own peril (and their peril as well). As Fox and Levin (2001, 87) have wisely remarked, "Complacency would be a terrible mistake." We agree wholeheartedly. The only way to continue to reduce the delinquency rate is to focus on the welfare of our young people, especially the most vulnerable. An ounce of prevention, as the saying goes, is worth a pound of cure.

Having dispelled some common misperceptions, we begin our review of facts and figures by examining juvenile population demographics. This will be followed by a look at juvenile offenders. We then discuss recent trends in the juvenile justice system, before we examine findings on juveniles as victims as well as youth in crisis.

The Juvenile Population in the United States

In the United States, it is the responsibility of the U.S. Census Bureau to keep track of the nation's population. Every ten years in the United States, the Census Bureau conducts a massive count of the entire U.S. population. By looking at the resulting data, we can get a good sense of juvenile population demographics.

As of April 1, 2000, the United States had a population of about 281 million people (U.S. Census Bureau). About one-fourth (26 percent), or 72 million people, were juveniles (i.e., under the age of eighteen). While the raw number of juveniles has increased since 1990, the percentage of juveniles in the U.S. population has stayed roughly the same. The percentage of elderly (especially those age sixty-five and older), on the other hand, is increasing rapidly. Current projections suggest that the juvenile population will increase by approximately 8 percent between 1995 and 2015, whereas the percentage of those persons age sixty-five and older will increase by about 36 percent during this same period of time (U.S. Census Bureau). This means that there will be proportionately more elderly and fewer juveniles. All things being equal, an older population is associated with a lower crime rate (Siegel and Senna 2000). This is, of course, potentially very good news.

Many observers of U.S. society call this demographic situation "the graying of America." One has to wonder what will happen to the well-being of U.S. youth as the population continues to age. Will support for juvenile programs (for example, day-care and after-school programs) and adequate funding for education be forthcoming? Whereas the elderly are politically well organized and powerful as a bloc of voters, juveniles are relatively powerless. Who will advocate for their needs? We do not believe in pitting one generation of Americans against another, but we realize that competition for finite resources is a fact of social and political life.

The graying of America notwithstanding, the youth population will continue to grow, at least in raw numbers, in coming years. In fact, today there are 40 million youngsters in the United States under the age of ten. This is the largest cohort of youngsters since the baby boom generation (baby boomers are those persons born between 1946 and 1964). As these youngsters—

sometimes called the baby boomerang generation (i.e., the children of baby boomers)—age, they will enter the crime-prone years of adolescence and early adulthood (Siegel and Senna 2000). With this increase in the population of teens, we might reasonably expect to witness an increase in the problems associated with youth, including delinquent behavior (Fox and Levin 2001). The changing age structure of the United States—in particular, the rapid growth in the percentage of elderly coupled with a large cohort of youngsters—makes it difficult to predict what will happen with crime rates in the future. On the one hand, an older population is usually associated with a lower crime rate. On the other hand, we have a very large group of youngsters entering into the crime-prone years. Will crime rates increase? Will they decrease? Or will these two demographic factors cancel each other out? There is no way to know for certain. We do know this, though: the prediction that juvenile crime rates would increase drastically at the end of the 1990s and early years of the twenty-first century has not materialized. Some researchers—for example, James A. Fox (1996)—have warned of a wave of youth crime. Fortunately, this has not come to pass. Indeed, the juvenile crime rate has declined in recent years. However, it may be the case that Fox is right; perhaps his prediction is accurate but off by a few years.

Turning our attention to the matters of social and racial inequality, we see that minorities are overrepresented in poverty statistics. Of the nearly 72 million juveniles in the United States today, about three-fourths (79 percent) are classified as white (this includes many Hispanics) and 21 percent are nonwhite. The juveniles most likely to be living in poverty, however, are nonwhites, particularly African Americans. In fact, African American youth are about twice as likely as white youth to be poor (U.S. Census Bureau).

In addition to the risk of living in poverty, juveniles from minority groups are more likely to be arrested and more likely to be victims of crime and delinquency (Snyder and Sickmund 1999). Race and social class are among the most powerful predictors of negative outcomes for youth in the United States.

Another growing problem with minority and poor youth is school dropout rates. Minority youth in the United States also have a significantly greater risk of failing in school. Unfortunately, many of the social problems facing our young people have become self-perpetuating. That is, poverty breeds more poverty, poor academic performance leads to more of the same, and as a result, social problems get handed down from one generation to the next like a macabre family heirloom. When it comes to life chances—that is, the likelihood that one will be rich or poor, attend a good school or a bad school, be arrested or be the victim of a crime—race and social class matter.

What does this all mean? First, these demographic factors alone should prompt us to be sensitive toward the problems faced by young people. The large cohort of youngsters who are quickly becoming teenagers may spell trouble. That is, the recent decreases in the delinquency rate may soon end and we may witness a new wave of serious delinquency. Second, the segment of the juvenile population that is increasing the fastest (i.e., minorities) is the same group suffering from the most serious risk factors (e.g., poverty, single-parent family composition). Taken together, these two factors should prompt us to institute massive prevention programs aimed at the most at-risk youth. If we fail to care for the most vulnerable members of society, we face the possibility of a resurgence of serious youth crime.

Juvenile Offenders: Arrest Statistics

We begin this section by posing some questions: How many juveniles are arrested each year in the United States? For what types of offenses are they most likely to be arrested? Do boys commit more offenses than girls? Do minorities commit more delinquent acts than whites? Are most acts of delinquency violent? Is serious and violent delinquency on the rise or is it declining? Is drug use among young people on the rise? It is to these and related questions that we next turn our attention. First, however, a few words about the various ways delinquent behavior can be measured—for example, arrest statistics, victim surveys, self-reports, and cohort studies—are in order.

It turns out that measuring delinquent behavior is not as easy as it might at first seem. Criminologists and others who study juvenile delinquency have recognized for some time now that there are serious limitations and inherent problems in measuring illegal behavior. As just one example, while the police make millions of arrests each year, there are many more acts of crime and delinquency that do not result in arrest. In fact, many criminal and delinquent acts are never reported to the police. Why, one might reasonably ask, does this occur? Is it possible that the victim of a crime or delinquent act would fail to contact the police? The answer is, surprisingly, yes.

There are several reasons why some crimes are not reported to the police. For one, some victims of crime may figure that there is little the police can actually do. Imagine the case in which a lawn mower and gas can have been stolen from your backyard and no one witnessed the act. In such a situation, you, the homeowner, may rightly conclude that the police stand little chance of actually catching the person responsible for this theft.

Fear of retaliation is another reason some crimes are never reported. Put yourself in the place of an elderly woman living next store to a bunch of young and rowdy gang members who routinely drink, smoke marijuana, fight, play their music loud, and vandalize neighbors' property. In such a case, the elderly woman may fear that calling the police will only result in more trouble. In fact, in some communities a large crowd of people may witness a brutal crime (e.g., rape or murder); however, the police may not be able to find anyone willing to come forward and testify against the assailants. Fear of retaliation leads to the problem of "seeing but not seeing."

Still other victims of crime may decide not to contact the police because they are themselves involved in criminal behavior. If a drug dealer is robbed and beaten by a rival drug dealer, it is unlikely that the police will be contacted. For all of these reasons, then, police arrest statistics represent only the tip of the crime iceberg. Unreported crime represents what some criminologists call the "dark figures of crime." In order to get at these dark figures, criminologists have devised self-report surveys and victim surveys. We will look at self-report and victim data after we examine police arrest statistics.

The limitations of police data notwithstanding, arrest statistics still have important stories to tell. As indicated below in Table 5.1, U.S. police made more than 13.9 million arrests in 2000. Of these, more than 2.2 million were for serious or "index" crimes. Four offenses—murder, aggravated assault, robbery, and rape—make up the violent crime index. Four other offenses—arson, burglary, larceny-theft, and motor vehicle theft—make up the property crime index. Taken together, these eight offenses comprise the total crime index, or the crimes considered by the FBI to be among the most serious of all crimes.

Table 5.1
Arrests in the United States, 2000

	Number of Arrests	Percentage Juvenile Arrested
Violent index crime arrests	625,132	15.9
Property index crime arrests	1,620,928	32
Total index crime arrests	2,246,054	27.5
Total crime arrests (index and nonindex crimes)	13,980,297	17.1

Source: Federal Bureau of Investigation. Adapted by authors.

As shown in Table 5.1, juveniles accounted for approximately one-sixth (15.9 percent) of all the arrests for violent index crimes, about one-third (32 percent) of property index crimes, more than one-fourth (27.5 percent) of all index crimes, and slightly less than one-fifth (17.1 percent) of all crimes (index and nonindex offenses combined). When you consider that juveniles account for about one-fourth (26 percent) of the U.S. population, it becomes clear that they are overrepresented in property index arrests and total index arrests, but they are underrepresented in violent index arrests and total (index and nonindex) arrests.

Do juveniles commit most of the crime in the United States? The answer is clearly no. However, most crime in the United States—at least index crime—is committed by people under age twenty-five (i.e., older teens and young adults). FBI arrest data for 2000 reveal that 55.1 percent of all those arrested for index crimes were under age twenty-five. As some observers of crime and delinquency have argued, crime is a young person's game. On average, property crime arrests peak at about age 16, whereas violent crime arrests peak later at age eighteen (Siegel and Senna 2000). Therefore, street crime in the United States is committed disproportionately by young people, although not all of them are juveniles (that is, under the legal age).

Looking more closely at the arrests of juveniles in the United States, we see that the offense for which juveniles are most likely to be arrested is larceny-theft. As Table 5.2 reveals, juveniles are far more likely to be arrested for a property crime than a violent crime. Furthermore, males are much more likely than females to

Table 5.2
Juvenile Arrests in the United States, 2000

Offense Charged	Number of Male Arrests (%)	Number of Female Arrests (%)
Murder	610 (89.3)	73 (10.7)
Forcible rape	2,588 (98.9)	29 (1.1)
Robbery	14,742 (90.6)	1,535 (9.4)
Aggravated assault	30,299 (77)	9,049 (23)
Violent crime index	48,169 (81.8)	10,686 (18.2)
Burglary	50,535 (88)	6,890 (12)
Larceny-theft	140,363 (63)	82,594 (37)
Motor vehicle theft	23,344 (82.9)	4,804 (17.1)
Arson	4,574 (88.4)	600 (11.6)
Property crime index	218,816 (69.8)	94,888 (30.2)
Total crime index	266,985 (71.7)	105,574 (28.3)

Source: Federal Bureau of Investigation. Adapted by authors.

be arrested, particularly for violent crimes. However, females are increasingly involved in delinquent behavior, including violent behavior.

Is most delinquent behavior violent? The answer, once again, is no. There were fewer than 700 juvenile arrests for murder in 2000, compared to more than 220,000 juvenile arrests for larceny-theft. Most delinquency tends to be minor, and most delinquent acts involve property crime, not violent crime. This is a consistent research finding. However, there is a group of juvenile offenders—variously referred to as serious habitual offenders, the chronic few, chronic offenders, or career criminals—who are different from most other juvenile offenders in some important ways. We will look at the chronic few later in this chapter.

In addition to the gender difference in juvenile arrests, researchers have known for some time now that minority youth, especially black youth, are much more likely than their white peers to be arrested, particularly for serious crimes (for example,

**Figure 5.1 Percentage of Juvenile Arrests for Index
Offenses by African Americans, 1999**

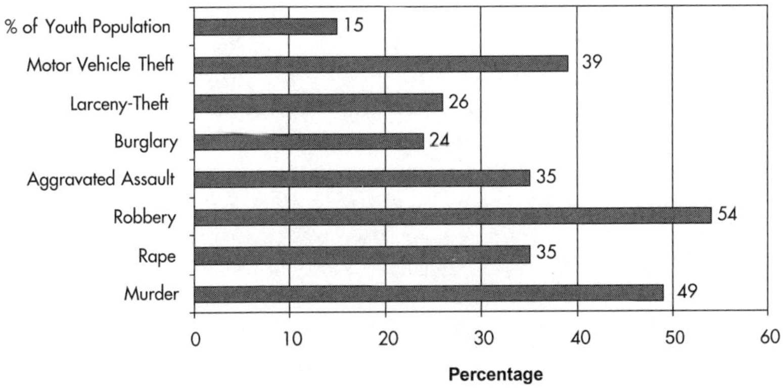

Source: Federal Bureau of Investigation. Adapted by author.

index offenses). Figure 5.1 provides evidence of this phenomenon for the year 1999. As you are examining Figure 5.1, keep in
mind that in 1999 about 15 percent of the youth population in the
United States was African American. According to arrest statistics, black youth are highly overrepresented in serious delinquent behavior.

The data in Figure 5.1 are troubling. In 1999, black youth
represent more than half (54 percent) of all the juvenile arrests for
robbery, nearly half (49 percent) of the juvenile arrests for murder, and more than a third (35 percent) of the juvenile arrests for
rape and aggravated assault.

What do the data in Figure 5.1 really mean? That black
youth are indeed more delinquent, more violent, than their white
peers? That agents of the criminal justice system, particularly the
police, are biased toward black youth? Is there actually little difference in behavior between white and black youth? Do the police and others (e.g., prosecutors, judges, probation officers) simply single out minorities?

In general, delinquency researchers have concluded that
there is some truth in each of these positions. It appears that minority youth, particularly those living in the most impoverished
areas or ghettos, are more violent than juveniles residing in
higher-income neighborhoods. Some researchers (e.g., Anderson
1999) now refer to inner-city neighborhoods as "ground zero"

because violence in these areas has become a common and tragic way of life for many disaffected youth. These neighborhoods are, in many ways, war zones.

There is other evidence, however, that the police and others in the juvenile justice system do, in fact, treat juveniles differentially depending on race and social class (Miller 1996; Office of Juvenile Justice and Delinquency Prevention; Reiman 2004; Sentencing Project). When these two factors are put together—grinding poverty leading to violence as a way of life coupled with biased treatment by the police and others in the criminal and juvenile justice system—the findings presented in Figure 5.1, though obviously tragic, begin to make sense.

There is another way to make sense of the data in Figure 5.1. As we will discuss later in the chapter, race makes little difference in many forms of delinquency, particularly relatively minor forms (often referred to as "garden-variety" delinquency). However, there is compelling evidence that race makes a significant difference in more serious acts of delinquency (for example, index offenses). Along with other researchers (e.g., Walker, Spohn, and DeLone 1996), we have come to believe that there are actually two delinquency and crime problems in the United States. The first of these problems, which can reasonably be called garden-variety delinquency, seems to cut across racial lines. Both white and nonwhite youth commit relatively minor to moderate acts of delinquency at a fairly high rate (we will discuss this in detail when we turn to self-report survey data). A look at the other delinquency problem, which can be termed serious and violent delinquency, shows race and social class as significant predictors, with low-income and minority youth committing crimes such as robbery, aggravated assault, and murder at a higher rate than other groups.

Delinquency and juvenile justice are embedded within a larger social structural and cultural context. It has long been recognized that the U.S. experience (i.e., what it is like to live in U.S. society) varies widely according to one's background, location, and the like. For some, the experience is relatively safe and comfortable; this is the United States that is experienced by the middle class (including middle-class blacks). For others, however, the experience includes violence, poverty, and blocked opportunities on a daily basis. This is the United States that is disproportionately experienced by minorities (and poor whites). With this

**Figure 5.2 Juvenile Arrest Rate for Violent Index Crimes
(Murder, Rape, Robbery, Aggravated Assault)
1980 – 2000**

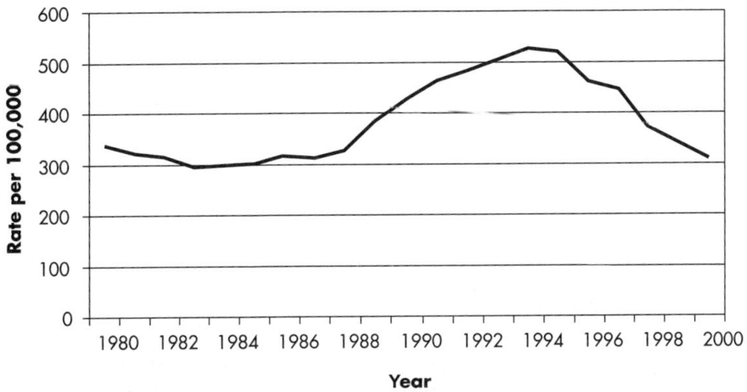

Source: OJJDP. Adapted by authors.

duality of experience in mind, it should come as little surprise that there are two different delinquency problems.

The data presented thus far provide a snapshot of juvenile arrests for a single point in time. While this is useful information, it tells us nothing about longer-term patterns or trends. Figure 5.2 shows that serious, violent delinquency (as measured by arrests for murder, rape, aggravated assault, and robbery) increased sharply between 1988 and 1994. Since 1994, however, this trend has reversed.

What happened between the late 1980s and the mid-1990s? What can explain the dramatic increase in youth violence? While there are a number of possible answers to this question, there is growing agreement among criminologists that two factors—crack cocaine and handguns—are responsible for much of the youth violence that occurred during this period (Blumstein 1995). Crack, a cheap and smokable form of cocaine, devastated many neighborhoods during the late 1980s and early 1990s. Juveniles, particularly those from low-income areas, found the lure of fast money from "clocking," or selling crack cocaine, to be almost irresistible (Anderson 1999). Crack dealing is an exceptionally violent business. When there is a dispute, dealers and buyers are not able to turn to the police or another legitimate authority. Instead, disputes are settled privately, often with the aid of a gun. Fortunately, by the early 1990s, as crack markets stabilized and rates of crack use declined, the associated youth violence also decreased.

Kids and Guns

Research shows us that guns, particularly handguns, are a significant problem. Indeed, it has been well established that easy access to handguns is one of the most significant contributors to the increase in juvenile violence and homicide in the United States between 1988 and 1994 (Blumstein 1995). Handguns continue to be a problem, as evidenced by more recent studies. For example, in 1999 there were approximately 28,000 juvenile arrests for weapons-related charges, and more than six out of every ten juvenile homicides were committed with a gun (Siegel 2002, 29). Further, we know that the problem of juvenile suicide (to be discussed in some detail later in this chapter) is closely tied to guns. Snyder and Swahn (2004) report that of the nearly 21,000 confirmed juvenile suicides in the United States between 1981 and 1998, almost two-thirds (62 percent) were committed with a gun.

Our own experiences in working with juveniles over the years have taught us that weapons in general, and guns in particular, are a major contributor to youth violence. Disagreements that would normally result in a shouting match or perhaps a fistfight all too easily turn deadly when guns are added to the situation. Clearly, too, the well-publicized tragedies of Littleton, Colorado; Jonesboro, Arkansas; Paducah, Kentucky; and Pearl, Mississippi (all sites of school shootings) would not have happened if the juvenile killers did not have access to guns. Several questions come to mind regarding juveniles and handguns: How common is it for juveniles to possess guns? Where and how do young people get guns? Why are they drawn to guns?

Social scientific studies reveal that juvenile weapons possession is more widespread than many realize. For example, a recent study by the Centers for Disease Control (Centers for Disease Control 2004) found that nationwide 17.1 percent of students reported carrying a weapon (which includes a gun, knife, or club) on at least one occasion during the thirty days before being surveyed. Male students were about four times more likely to have carried a weapon than were females (26.9 percent versus 6.7 percent). This same study also found that 6.1 percent of students reported they had carried a gun at least once during the thirty days preceding the survey. Again, males (10.2 percent) were more likely than females (1.6 percent) to carry a gun.

The problem of gun possession and violence is much greater in inner-city communities (Lizotte and Sheppard 2001). Many urban areas have become virtual war zones, the sound of gunfire a regular part of the local landscape. The combination of poverty, easy access to guns, a thriving drug trade, and an emergent "code of the street" has led to unprecedented levels of juvenile violence (Anderson 1999; Beckett and Sasson 2004).

Obviously, guns present a real and significant danger, especially when they are in the hands of impulsive youngsters. Besides the obvious risk that guns pose, research reveals that other dangerous and criminal behaviors "cluster" with gun possession. The National Longitudinal Survey of Youth (as reported in Snyder and Sickmund 1999) found that gun-carrying youth are more likely than other youth to be involved in drug use and drug dealing, to belong to a gang, and to have engaged in violent criminal behavior. Thus, guns are a real and immediate danger, as well as an indicator that other dangers are present.

How do youngsters gain access to guns? Our own and other research makes clear, obtaining a gun is not particularly difficult. Approximately one in two U.S. households has one or more guns, so many youth are able to get a gun from their own homes. In addition, juveniles steal guns, borrow guns from friends, or purchase them on the black market.

We have discussed the prevalence of juvenile gun possession and its relationship to violence, as well as the problem of easy access. Still the question remains, why do juveniles carry and use guns? Juveniles are drawn to guns for several reasons, including what we call the "four p's": protection, prestige (that is, gaining status among peers), profit (the gun is a tool of the drug trade), and power.

When one of the authors (Wolfe) was working in a juvenile detention center, he learned that guns are incredibly important to some youngsters. He observed, for example, that juveniles would carve replicas out of bars of soap or fashion them out of paper and tape. Occasionally, residents would get a copy of a hunting or sporting magazine that had gun advertisements and would hang pictures of guns on their wall, much like other young men might hang pictures of bikini-clad models. In our interviews with young people, no other topic was as interesting to them as guns. When we would ask questions about types of guns, availability of guns, and use of guns, the youngsters tended to become excited and animated. They could talk for extended periods of times about the relative advantages of this type of gun or that type of ammunition.

The first "p" we discuss is protection. About the protection guns offer, one young man reported, "When you live in my neighborhood, you gotta carry a gun. If you don't you might get caught sleepin' [being unprepared]." Other typical comments included such statements as "I feel like nothin' can hurt me when I got my nine [9mm handgun] with me." Still others reported, "If you don't have a gun, you won't be able to defend yourself" (Wolfe 1996).

The second "p" is for prestige. One young man reported that "people be lookin' up to me when I'm strapped [armed]." Not only does prestige come from carrying a gun, but it can be greatly increased when a youngster demonstrates his willingness to use a gun. A young man known as Tippy reported to us that "everybody respects you when you got a reputation for heart [bravery]. People in my hood know that I will bust a cap [shoot] in a second." Another youngster told us, "When I'm strapped I'm hopin' somebody will beef [argue] with me, so I can let him know what time it is" (Wolfe 1996).

The third "p" is for profit. Other comments about guns taught us that guns are a tool in the drug trade. As one crack dealer told us, "You gotta carry a gun if you are in the business [drug dealing]. If you don't, somebody is gonna gank [rob] you." Others would state that you can't be in the "dope game" unless you carry a gun. Thus, guns can be viewed as a tool for profit (Wolfe 1996).

The fourth—and the most important—"p" is for power. We have been told by a variety of youth that having a gun makes them feel powerful. Some have described an almost euphoric sensation that accompanies the carrying of a gun. What is particularly frightening is that some youth have reported to us that shooting a gun at someone provides an even greater sense of power and a better "high." One young man told us that he loves to pull a gun on someone just to see them get scared and that he really "gets off" when he shoots at them. He reported, "I love to see them get so scared that they almost s*** their pants." More commonly, we have heard juveniles say that they "feel like nothin' and nobody in the world can mess with me when I'm packin' [carrying a gun]." Some youth have told us that they actually look forward to someone harassing them when they are carrying a gun so that they can "put the a**hole in his place" (Wolfe 1996).

The problem with guns is greater than their easy availability. We believe that it is important not only to get guns out of the hands of young people but also to get guns out of their hearts and minds. When juveniles feel safe, perhaps carrying a gun will be viewed as unnecessary. When juveniles find legitimate and prosocial opportunities to feel good about themselves, when they are able to establish a positive sense of self without resorting to crime, and when they can find decent jobs, perhaps the lure of guns will be lessened. And, most important, when we as a society decide that we can empower youngsters in healthy ways, perhaps the power of the gun will be less compelling.

Having examined delinquent behavior based on police arrest statistics, we now turn our attention to research findings based on self-reports. As the name makes clear, self-report data provide information about offending based on the reports (in interview or survey form) of juveniles themselves.

Self-Report Data

Criminologists have devised several ways to measure delinquent behavior. In addition to arrest statistics, self-report surveys can be used to gauge the nature and extent of delinquent behavior. These surveys ask a representative sample of juveniles to report on their involvement in various forms of delinquent behavior. One of the most well-known and -respected examples of self-report research is the Monitoring the Future survey. Since 1975, this national survey of youth has been conducted annually by researchers at the University of Michigan's Institute for Social Research. Each year, some 50,000 young people are surveyed to determine their attitudes, opinions, and behaviors.

Researchers have learned a great deal from this type of research. For one thing, we now know that there is far more delinquent behavior among U.S. youth than ever reaches the attention

Table 5.3
Self-Report Delinquency by U.S. High School Seniors, 2000
(percentage reporting committing delinquent
act at least once in the past 12 months)

Delinquent Act	White Youth	Black Youth
Taking part in a fight between two groups	18.8%	17.8%
Hurting someone badly enough they needed bandages or medical attention	10.8%	14.0%
Using a knife, gun, or some other weapon to take something from someone	1.7%	4.6%
Taking something not belonging to you worth under $50	30.6%	25.7%
Taking something not belonging to you worth over $50	10.6%	13.0%

Source: Sourcebook of Criminal Justice Statistics Online. Adapted by authors.

of law enforcement officials. Further, youth from all backgrounds, not just inner-city minority youth, engage in delinquent behavior. Table 5.3 provides data on several types of self-reported delinquent behavior.

Table 5.3 shows little difference between white and black high school seniors in self-reported delinquency. For example, it shows that about 18 percent of both white and black youth reported that they had taken part in a fight between two groups. Looking at minor theft, we see that 30.6 percent of white juveniles and 25.7 percent of black juveniles reported that they had taken something not belonging to them worth less than $50. Black youth were somewhat more likely to report that they had stolen something worth more than $50; they were also somewhat more likely to say that they had hurt someone enough to require a bandage or medical attention (this represents assault). A larger percentage of black high school seniors (4.6 percent compared to 1.7 percent for whites) admitted that they had used a weapon to take something from someone (armed robbery).

Table 5.4
Lifetime Prevalence of Drug Use for 8th, 10th, and 12th Graders

	1991	1992	1993	1994	1995	1996	1997	1998	1999	2000
Any illicit drug										
8th grade	18.7%	20.6%	22.5%	25.7%	28.5%	31.2%	29.4%	29.0%	28.3%	26.8%
10th grade	30.6%	29.8%	32.8%	37.4%	40.9%	45.4%	47.3%	44.9%	46.2%	45.6%
12th grade	44.1%	40.7%	42.9%	45.6%	48.4%	50.8%	54.3%	54.1%	54.7%	54.0%
Marijuana										
8th grade	10.2%	11.2%	12.6%	16.7%	19.9%	23.1%	22.6%	22.2%	22.0%	20.3%
10th grade	23.4%	21.4%	24.4%	30.4%	34.1%	39.8%	42.3%	39.6%	40.9%	40.3%
12th grade	36.7%	32.6%	35.3%	38.2%	41.7%	44.9%	49.6%	49.1%	49.7%	48.8%
Cocaine										
8th grade	2.3%	2.9%	2.9%	3.6%	4.2%	4.5%	4.4%	4.6%	4.7%	4.5%
10th grade	4.1%	3.3%	3.6%	4.3%	5.0%	6.5%	7.1%	7.2%	7.7%	6.9%
12th grade	7.8%	6.1%	6.1%	5.9%	6.0%	7.1%	8.7%	9.3%	9.8%	8.6%
Heroin										
8th grade	1.2%	1.4%	1.4%	2.0%	2.3%	2.4%	2.1%	2.3%	2.3%	1.9%
10th grade	1.2%	1.2%	1.3%	1.5%	1.7%	2.1%	2.1%	2.3%	2.3%	2.2%
12th grade	0.9%	1.2%	1.1%	1.2%	1.6%	1.8%	2.1%	2.0%	2.0%	2.4%
Ecstasy										
8th grade	—	—	—	—	—	3.4%	3.2%	2.7%	2.7%	4.3%
10th grade	—	—	—	—	—	5.6%	5.7%	5.1%	6.0%	7.3%
12th grade	—	—	—	—	—	6.1%	6.9%	5.8%	8.0%	11.0%

Note: "—" indicates data not available.
Source: Monitoring the Future. Adapted by authors.

The data in Table 5.3 show two things: (1) in general, the gap in self-reported delinquency between white and black youth is not wide, and (2) even in self-report data we find some racial differences regarding the most violent kinds of crime (that is, robbery and assault).

Table 5.4 provides self-report data on one specific type of delinquent behavior, drug use. The results show that a significant percentage of juveniles have used illegal drugs. An examination of drug use trends is important because drug use is often associated with other forms of delinquent behavior.

Several findings from Table 5.4 are worth mentioning. For one, marijuana is clearly the illicit drug of choice for most youngsters. In 2000, more than one-fifth (20.3 percent) of eighth graders reported that they had used marijuana at least once. For tenth and twelfth graders, the results are 40.3 percent and 48.8 percent, respectively. Second, the results show the use of any illicit drug for all three grades was higher in 2000 than in 1991. This increase in drug use followed a lengthy period of declining use by young people (from the late 1970s through the early 1990s). Finally, there is reason to be concerned about the recent appearance and rapid rise in the use of MDMA, or ecstasy, as it is better known.

The connection between drugs and delinquency is one of the most consistent and robust in all of the research literature. For one thing, the use of drugs is itself a type of delinquent act. For example, underage drinking and underage tobacco use are both status offenses. The use of illicit drugs (e.g., marijuana, cocaine, etc.) represents delinquent or criminal acts. Moreover, youth who use intoxicating drugs are much more likely to be involved in other forms of delinquency. Drug use and delinquency cluster together.

The data in Tables 5.3 and 5.4 provide us with some sense of the extent of self-reported delinquency. There are several other key lessons to learn from self-report surveys. For one, these studies have revealed that white and middle-class youth are just as likely as nonwhite and lower-class youth to engage in garden-variety delinquency. Second, self-report studies have shown us that there is considerably more delinquent behavior in our society than is ever reported to the authorities. And finally, self-report studies have taught us that there has not been a major increase or a major decrease in delinquency. Instead, these findings suggest that delinquency, at least in its most common forms, is consistent from year to year.

A final issue regarding this research is the contradictory findings in police arrest data and self-report data. Specifically, why do police data show that nonwhites are more likely to engage in delinquency when self-report data do not show this same outcome? Our best understanding of this complicated and controversial topic is that police data tend to deal with more serious forms of delinquency (e.g., robbery, rape, murder, and aggravated assault), whereas self-report data tend to deal with less serious forms of delinquency.

In essence, comparing police data and self-report data is like comparing apples and oranges. We believe, along with many other researchers, that serious delinquency is more of a problem with minority youth, especially lower-income juveniles, because they are most likely to experience grinding poverty, profound alienation, and a commitment to the "code of the street" (i.e., willingness to commit violence).

We also know from cohort studies that a small number of juveniles are responsible for a tremendous amount of serious and violent delinquency. By following large groups of juveniles over extended periods of time (often several decades), researchers have found that a small group of juvenile offenders, the "chronic few" (perhaps as small as 6 percent of the juvenile population), commit most of the serious and violent crime in a community (Wolfgang, Figlio, and Sellin 1972). The factors that seem to separate or distinguish chronic juvenile offenders from others are the following:

- Early onset. The chronic few display behavioral problems as early as elementary school.
- Race. Minority youth, particularly African American youth, are much more likely to become chronic offenders.
- Education. Chronic offenders are much more likely to experience trouble at school and academic failure.
- Poverty. Chronic offenders are more likely to come from low-income families living in areas of concentrated poverty.
- Gender. Boys are considerably more likely to be chronic offenders. The reason for this is not fully understood at this time. It is likely a combination of socialization experiences (we raise boys differently in our culture than we do girls) and biological differences.

Garden-variety or less-serious delinquents, on the other hand, come from all social class, racial, ethnic, and other types of backgrounds. Most juvenile offenders engage in mundane, minor forms of delinquency, such as status offenses, simple drug possession, and petty property crimes.

To summarize, delinquent behavior can be measured in several ways. The primary sources of delinquency data include arrest statistics, self-report surveys, and victimization surveys. Data from arrests statistics and self-reports show that serious delinquency increased from the late 1980s to the mid-1990s. Since

1994, there has been a steady and sharp decrease in serious delinquency. Further, certain groups are more likely to be involved in serious delinquency: namely, males and lower-income minorities. Finally, garden-variety delinquency is fairly widespread and cuts across race and class lines. We now turn our attention to research on recent trends in juvenile court and juvenile corrections.

Trends in Juvenile Justice

In this section, we will examine juvenile court and juvenile corrections data. More specifically, we will present information on the number of juveniles sentenced to probation, the number sent to residential placement (incarcerated), the number of juveniles waived or transferred to the adult system, and the number of juveniles who have been given the death penalty.

Figure 5.3 shows that the number of juveniles placed on probation increased throughout the 1990s. In 1990 approximately 221,000 juveniles received a disposition (sentence) of probation. In 1999, almost 400,000 juveniles were placed on probation, which continues to be the workhorse of the juvenile justice system. However, many juveniles are placed in institutions. Juveniles receiving a disposition of "residential placement" increased from about 125,000 in 1990 to approximately 156,000 in 1999. While there is clearly a need to incarcerate some very dangerous and disturbed juvenile offenders, juvenile institutions are generally viewed by experts as less effective than community-based alternatives.

One of the greatest concerns regarding juvenile institutions is the disproportionate number of minority and low-income youth in such facilities. This concern has resulted in a program developed by the Office of Juvenile Justice and Delinquency Prevention (OJJDP) that is known as the Disproportionate Minority Confinement (DMC) initiative. The main goal of this program is to find ways to reduce the overrepresentation of minority youth in juvenile institutions.

As we mentioned in earlier chapters, waiver or transfer is a controversial and growing practice in the juvenile justice system. Waiver or transfer refers to the reassignment of a juvenile from the jurisdiction of the juvenile court system to the jurisdiction of the adult criminal court system. In recent years, a num-

**Figure 5.3 Number of Juveniles Placed on
Probation or Sentenced to a Residential Placement
(Incarcerated), 1990 – 1999**

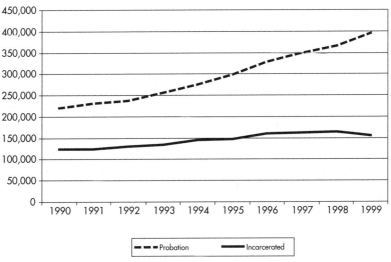

Source: OJJDP. Adapted by authors.

ber of states have made it easier to transfer juveniles. It is not
possible to determine the number of juveniles who have been
waived to the adult system with much precision or confidence,
as "there are no all-encompassing national data collected" on
this issue (Sentencing Project). However, what data are available
suggest that waivers are on the rise. For example, Snyder and
Sickmund (1999, 170) report a 47 percent increase in waivers between 1987 and 1996. As with arrest statistics, youth from lower-
income families, minorities, and males are overrepresented in
waiver statistics.

    If it turns out that waiver is an effective method to reduce
delinquency, then it is a reasonable course of action. The available research evidence, however, suggests that waiver may actually backfire; that is, it may lead to more rather than less delinquency and crime. As the researchers at the Sentencing Project
report, "The imposition of adult punishments, far from deterring
crime, actually increases the likelihood that a young person will
commit further criminal offenses. The transfer of increasing
numbers of children from juvenile to criminal courts is continu-

ing in the face of mounting evidence of the harm it does both to the children and to public safety" (Sentencing Project).

Another trend in juvenile justice involves the use of shock incarceration programs, which are probably better known as boot camps. The idea behind these programs is to shock the juvenile into realizing that he or she is in serious trouble. Another goal of the programs is to get tough with youthful offenders so that they will turn their lives around. By using a military-style approach—with an emphasis on strenuous physical activity, aggressive drill sergeants, and "in your face" tactics—program directors hope that the juvenile will become more responsible, more disciplined, and less likely to reoffend.

While boot camps are popular with policy makers and members of the public, the available research evidence offers little reason to be optimistic about the effectiveness of these programs to reduce recidivism (Regoli and Hewitt 2003, 404). In addition to being relatively ineffective in reducing recidivism rates, boot camps are controversial because they are expensive; there have also been reports that they can be abusive to juveniles.

Juveniles and the Death Penalty

Over the years, court rulings have allowed juveniles to be sentenced to death. Victor Streib (1998) reports that approximately 350 juvenile offenders had been executed since 1642. This works out to about 2 percent of all executions in the United States over the past 350 or so years. In addition, Streib's study found that all juveniles on death row in the early 2000s were males who had been convicted of murder. Over half of these inmates were minorities and nearly half were African American. Streib found that since 1976, twenty-one males had been executed for crimes committed when they were juveniles.

In 2002, when the juvenile death penalty was still considered constitutional, Streib found that there were eighty inmates on death row throughout the country who were sixteen or seventeen years old when they committed their crimes. This figure is still around 2 percent of the total death row population, which suggests that the death penalty for juveniles was still being imposed in similar proportions to all death sentences given in the United States in the 1990s ("Juveniles and the Death Penalty" 2004).

From 1989 to 2005, the U.S. Supreme Court ruled that executions were only constitutional for juveniles who were at least age sixteen at the time the offense was committed. On March 1, 2005, however, in a 5–4 ruling, the Supreme Court declared this practice unconstitutional. No one under the age of eighteen at the time the offense was committed can be executed for a crime.

The only other countries that have executed juveniles (under the age of eighteen) since 1990 are the Democratic Republic of the Congo, Iran, Nigeria, Pakistan, Saudi Arabia, and Yemen. More than 100 nations have laws that specifically forbid execution of juvenile offenders (Siegel and Senna 2000, 584; "Juveniles and the Death Penalty" 2004). In June 2002, in the case of *Atkins v. Virginia*, the U.S. Supreme Court outlawed the execution of mentally retarded offenders, although the specific definition of retardation for this purpose has not been clearly delineated for all jurisdictions that allow the death penalty, and such specification may not be forthcoming from the Court. Furthermore, the issue of when retardation occurs is also working its way through the courts as this book is being written. For example, in a current case in Virginia (that of Percy Walton), a psychiatrist concluded in a report filed in court on February 23, 2004, that Mr. Walton understood the consequences of his actions to the extent that he was aware of his pending execution (for a triple murder in 1996) and of his sentence to be executed for his conviction (by a guilty plea) of those murders. This judgment was reached by the psychiatrist despite the decline in Walton's IQ from 90 in 1996 to 66 in May 2003 and despite the reported comments made by the offender to the psychiatrist that he believed he would be able to come back to earth after his execution and work at a Burger King restaurant (Kahn 2004). It is expected that if the court upholds this psychiatrist's judgment, Mr. Walton's defense lawyers will file an appeal.

Juveniles as Victims

We now turn our attention to research on juveniles as victims of crime and delinquency. As we will show, many of the same factors that predict involvement in serious delinquency also predict

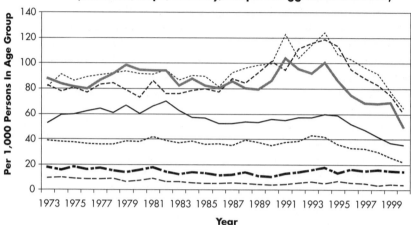

Figure 5.4 Violent Victimization Rate by Age, 1973 – 2000 (Homicide, Rape, Robbery, Simple & Aggravated Assault)

Source: U.S. Department of Justice, Bureau of statistics. Adapted by authors.

Key:
- ——— 25 to 34
- - - - - 12 to 15
- ······ 35 to 49
- ······ 16 to 19
- ▬ ▬ 50 to 64
- ▬▬ 20 to 24
- – – - 65+

the likelihood of a juvenile being the victim of a serious crime. While it is fairly well known that juveniles are overrepresented in arrest data, what is not as well known is the consistent finding that juveniles are overrepresented in victim data. That is to say, juveniles are more likely to be the victims of crime, particularly violent crime, than are older Americans. Let us take a look at some of the most recent findings regarding juveniles as victims.

As Figure 5.4 shows, juveniles and young adults are much more likely to be victims of violent crime than are older Americans. For example, those under age twenty-five are almost twice as likely as those twenty-five and older to be victims of homicide, rape, assault, and robbery. As we noted earlier, serious and violent crimes are disproportionately committed by young adults and juveniles, and young adults and juveniles are similarly overrepresented in serious and violent crime victimization statistics.

Other risk factors for crime victimization include gender (males are more likely to be the victims of most crimes), race (minorities are disproportionately the victims of serious crime), and location (people residing in urban areas are more likely to be crime victims than are suburbanites and those residing in rural locations).

The National Crime Victimization Survey and other victimization studies have revealed other important patterns in crime and delinquency victimization. Such patterns include the following (see Snyder and Sickmund 1999):

- Much youth violence is intraracial (e.g., white on white and black on black).
- Students are actually safer at school than away from school grounds.
- School-related crime has not increased in recent years.
- Most juvenile victimizations are not reported to authorities.
- Juvenile victims often know the person who victimized them.
- Juveniles face the greatest risk of victimization at the end of the school day and before parents return home from work in the evening (i.e., during periods of little or no adult supervision).

As researchers have learned, offenders and crime victims have many characteristics in common. Both groups contain disproportionate numbers of juveniles in general, and nonwhite, male, and low-income youth in particular. Victimization, like delinquent behavior, also appears to be related to low levels of adult supervision.

Youth in Crisis: Problems Facing Juveniles

Up to this point, we have focused our attention on juvenile demographics, juvenile offenders, juvenile justice system trends, and juveniles as victims of crime. We will place all of these matters into a broader context by examining what some authors have termed the "youth in crisis" situation (Siegel 2002). When delinquency is considered in this broader context, a different picture emerges. One way to think about juvenile delinquency is in individualistic terms. Juvenile offenders, according to this view, are simply bad people who knowingly and willingly make bad choices. Perhaps this is true in some cases. We do not question the belief that young people have free will, and we recognize that we should all be held accountable for our actions.

However, there is another way to think about delinquency and, by extension, the best way to respond to it. In this view, delinquency can be thought of as a symptom or manifestation of the many social problems confronting young people today. Some sociologists, like Elijah Anderson (1999), believe that drug dealing, drug use, and violence are the results of poverty, alienation, and a loss of faith in conventional society and its institutions (for example, the criminal justice system). To put it plainly, for many youngsters there is little to lose and much to gain by breaking the law. While breaking the law can be considered a choice that is freely made, it should be recognized that it can be a choice that makes the most sense to those who see few alternatives. By implication, if we want young people to make better decisions, we need to give them a good reason to do so. With this alternative view as a backdrop, we will examine three serious problems afflicting young people in the United States: suicide, school failure, and teen pregnancy. As you encounter the various facts and figures on these problems, think about how they might influence delinquent behavior.

How many juveniles commit suicide in the United States each year? Which juveniles are most likely to die at their own hands? Answers to these questions can be found in the research reports of two agencies: the National Center for Health Statistics (NCHS) and the Centers for Disease Control (CDC). Through data from the NCHS and the CDC, we know that there were 20,775 juveniles between the ages of seven and seventeen who committed suicide in the seventeen-year period between 1981 and 1998 (Snyder and Swahn 2004). This number is roughly equal to the number of juvenile homicide victims for this same time period. Think about this for just a moment: juveniles in the United States are almost as likely to die from suicide as from homicide. In fact, suicide is the fourth leading cause of death for juveniles over age six. The leading cause of death for this age group is unintentional injury (such as car crashes), while homicide and cancer are the second and third leading causes of death, respectively.

The risk for juvenile suicide is not spread evenly across the youth population; certain groups are at greater risk. Males are three times as likely as females to take their own lives. Race and ethnicity also make a difference in suicide risk. Native American youth are far more likely than any other group to commit suicide. Between 1981 and 1998, the suicide rate for this group was 57 per 1 million youth; for white youth the rate was 31 per 1 million; and for black youth it was 18 per 1 million (Snyder and Swahn 2004).

While a detailed discussion of these findings is beyond the scope of this book, we can offer some possible explanations based on the accumulated body of research on suicide. The reason that males commit suicide more often than females has to do mostly with the method used. That is, males are more likely to use a gun to commit suicide, whereas females are more likely to use less lethal means (such as pills). The reason that Native Americans have such a high risk for suicide is most likely due to the extreme deprivation they face, as well as the utter destruction of their culture. These explanations are telling, in that they show us once again that the choices people make (in this case the choice to end one's life) are influenced by structural (e.g., availability of guns) and cultural (e.g., loss of a traditional way of life) factors. It turns out, then, that juvenile suicide may not be simply a matter of people making bad choices (although we hasten to add that we think the choice to kill one's self is tragic and we should do everything we can as a society to prevent teen suicide).

Another serious problem facing young people is school failure. It may come as no surprise that many young people dislike school intensely. They are frustrated, alienated, and bored by formal education. For such students, school can be a major source of stress in their lives. One thing we know for sure is that low educational achievement is associated with a variety of bad outcomes, including delinquent behavior.

School failure can take a variety of forms. It may manifest itself in poor academic performance (that is, low grades or being held back), but it can also take the form of dropping out of school altogether. Data from the National Center for Education Statistics show that in 2001 about 1 in 10 (10.7 percent) Americans between the ages of sixteen and twenty-four could be classified as school dropouts (National Center for Education Statistics). Race and ethnicity are major determinants of these rates. For example, for whites the dropout rate in 2001 was 7.3 percent, while for blacks and Hispanics the rates were 10.9 percent and 27 percent, respectively.

Gender is also related to dropout rates. In 2001 the rate for males was 12.2 percent, while for females it was 9.3 percent. Although the dropout rates are cause for concern, there is some good news to report. In general, the dropout rate has been declining over the past thirty years. For example, in 1972 the overall dropout rate for sixteen- to twenty-four-year-olds was 14.6 percent. By 2001 that rate had dropped to 10.7 percent. A decline in the dropout rate has been experienced for all racial and ethnic groups. However, minority groups have continued to be overrepresented. One way to combat juvenile delinquency is to continue to work on lowering dropout rates.

A final problem we want to examine is teen pregnancy and teen births. Having a baby before one is prepared for such a huge responsibility can have life-altering effects. Whereas giving birth to and raising a child is stressful for most adults, the stress for teen parents must be compounded.

The accumulated evidence on the problem of teen pregnancy, fortunately, shows that the situation is improving. For example, in 1991 the birthrate for females between the ages of fifteen and nineteen was 6.2 percent (Centers for Disease Control 2003). By 2002 the rate for this age group had dropped to 4.3 percent.

The decline in teen pregnancies notwithstanding, there is still reason for concern. We know, for example, that race affects teen pregnancy rates. In 2002, the birthrate for white females between the ages of fifteen and nineteen was 2.9 percent. For black females in this age group, the rate was more than twice as high at 6.8 percent, while the rate for Hispanic females was even higher at 8.3 percent. So while the trend of decreasing teen births is encouraging, there is still much work to be done, especially with regard to minority female youth.

Summary and Conclusions

In this chapter we have covered a great deal of ground. We started off by dispelling some common misperceptions. Contrary to popular belief, delinquency is decreasing, not increasing. Most delinquency is minor, not violent mayhem committed by superpredators. The criminal justice system and the juvenile justice system are hardly soft on crime and delinquency. Unfortunately, Lady Justice is not blind—race and social class affect the kind of treatment one can get from the legal system.

We have noted that the juvenile population is growing. A large cohort of youngsters, sometimes referred to as the baby boomerang generation, will soon be entering the crime-prone years (teens and early twenties). It is hard to know if the delinquency rate will rise after almost a decade of decline. We have also shown that poverty, likely an important influence on serious delinquency, is concentrated among nonwhite youth. We argue that these two factors—an increasing juvenile population and a large number of at-risk youth—should motivate us as a society to step up our delinquency prevention and treatment efforts.

Although juveniles are indeed involved in a great deal of delinquent behavior, most of it is minor and mundane. Still, some juveniles (the so-called chronic few) engage in the most serious and violent forms of illicit behavior (e.g., murder, rape, and robbery). We would do well to act early and prevent trouble by directly attacking the risk factors associated with serious habitual offending.

We also discussed the lure that guns have for some juveniles and the widespread problem of juveniles carrying guns, particularly in inner-city communities. Fortunately, it is a problem that can be understood and thus dealt with successfully. We argue that guns will be less attractive when young people live in safe communities that provide them with healthy activities and opportunities. Young people, like all of us, want to be successful and they want to be good at something. When they have the chance to be successful in sports, music, theater, and the like, they will be less likely to turn to the street for validation.

Looking at recent trends, we showed that there is both good news and bad news. Homicides and other forms of serious delinquency (e.g., robbery and rape) committed by and against juveniles have declined over the past decade. However, there is reason to be concerned about an increase in drug use and its connection to delinquency. After many years of declining drug use by juveniles, we are once again seeing an increase. Of particular concern is the use of drugs such as MDMA (ecstasy) and heroin. A great deal of research demonstrates that there is a link between drug use and involvement in other forms of delinquent and criminal behavior.

Furthermore, while we do not want to be alarmists, we should be concerned about the potential for another wave of youth crime.

Ironically, while the juvenile crime rate has been falling, many states have been enacting more punitive (and ineffective) laws. While it is tempting to conclude that longer sentences, increasing transfers to the adult criminal justice system, and other similar "get tough" measures are responsible for the precipitous decline in juvenile crime, it is important to remember that the decline came before many of these tougher measures were adopted. Generally speaking, retributive justice is not a promising approach to solving our social problems.

We have also shown that juveniles are not only disproportionately involved in crime, they are overrepresented in victimization statistics. Research has revealed that offenders and victims share many characteristics; the most at-risk groups include young nonwhite males from urban areas.

Many problems—such as suicide, school failure, and teen pregnancy—continue to influence the lives of young people. While there are encouraging signs that some of these problems are on the decline, we still have much work to do. History teaches us that social problems may decrease, but they often increase after a period of time. Young people are our future. If we want them to be happy, healthy, and productive members of society, we must invest our resources in them.

All of these findings, taken together, provide us with important clues and insights into how we can best reduce delinquency and other social ills affecting our young people. As other researchers and authors have pointed out (for example, the landmark study by the University of Maryland [1997]), we must commit to putting our resources and energies where they are most needed. We have the knowledge and we know about programs that can improve the lives of young people; we know how to significantly reduce delinquency and victimization. It is a gross distortion to claim that we do not know what works to reduce delinquency. We know full well what needs to be done. What we need, more than anything else, is the social and political will to follow through and implement the policies and programs that have been demonstrated to work. If delinquency and related problems once again increase, we have no one to blame but ourselves.

References

Anderson, Elijah. 1999. *Code of the Street: Decency, Violence, and the Moral Life of the Inner City.* New York: W.W. Norton.

Beckett, Katherine, and Theodore Sasson. 2004. *Politics of Injustice: Crime and Punishment in America,* 2nd ed. Thousand Oaks, CA: Pine Forge.

Blumstein, Alfred. 1995. "Youth Violence, Guns, and the Illicit-Drug Industry." *Journal of Criminal Law and Criminology* 86: 10–36.

Centers for Disease Control. 2003. "Births: Final Data for 2002." *National Vital Statistics Reports,* December 17, 52(10).

———. 2004. *Surveillance Summaries,* May 21, MMWR 2004:53 (No. SS-2).

Federal Bureau of Investigation (FBI). http://www.fbi.gov/ucr/ucr.htm.

Fox, James A. 1996. *Trends in Juvenile Violence: A Report to the United States Attorney General on Current and Future Rates of Juvenile Offending.* Boston: Northeastern University.

Fox, James A., and Jack Levin. 2001. *The Will to Kill: Making Sense of Senseless Murder.* Boston: Allyn and Bacon.

"Juveniles and the Death Penalty." 2004. www.deathpenaltyinfo.org/juvchar.html.

Kahn, Chris. 2004. "Psychiatrist Says Killer Competent for Execution, Despite Mental Handicaps." *The Roanoke Times,* February 24, p. 7.

Lizotte, Alan, and David Sheppard. 2001. "Gun Use by Male Juveniles: Research and Prevention." *OJJDP JuvenileJustice Bulletin* (July).

Lundman, Richard J. 2001. *Prevention and Control of Juvenile Delinquency,* 3rd ed. New York: Oxford University Press.

Mauer, Marc. 1999. *Race to Incarcerate.* New York: New Press.

Miller, Jerome G. 1996. *Search and Destroy: African-American Males in the Criminal Justice System.* Cambridge: Cambridge University Press.

National Center for Education Statistics. http://nces.ed.gov.

Office of Juvenile Justice and Delinquency Prevention (OJJDP). http://ojjdp.ncjrs.org.

Regoli, Robert M., and John D. Hewitt. 2003. *Delinquency in Society,* 5th ed. New York: McGraw-Hill.

Reiman, Jeffrey. 2004. *Rich Get Richer and the Poor Get Prison: Ideology, Class, and Criminal Justice,* 7th ed. Boston: Pearson.

Sentencing Project. http://www.sentencingproject.org/brief/juveniles.html.

Siegel, Larry. 2002. *Juvenile Delinquency: The Core.* Belmont, CA: Wadsworth.

Siegel, Larry, and Joseph Senna. 2000. *Juvenile Delinquency: Theory, Practice, and Law,* 7th ed. Belmont, CA: Wadsworth.

Snyder, Howard N., and Melissa Sickmund. 1999. *Juvenile Offenders and Victims: 1999 National Report.* Washington, DC: Office of Juvenile Justice and Delinquency Prevention.

Snyder, Howard N., and Monica H. Swahn. 2004. *Juvenile Suicides, 1981–1998.* Washington, DC: Office of Juvenile Justice and Delinquency Prevention.

Sourcebook of Criminal Justice Statistics Online. http://www.albany.edu/sourcebook/1995/pdf/t362.pdf.

Streib, Victor L. 1998. "The Juvenile Death Penalty Today: Death Sentences and Executions for Juvenile Crimes, January 1973–October 1998." http://www.law.onu.edu/faculty/streib/juvdeath.pdf.

University of Maryland. 1997. "Preventing Crime: What Works, What Doesn't, What's Promising." Washington, DC: U.S. Government Printing Office.

U.S. Census Bureau. http://www.census.gov.

U.S. Department of Justice, Bureau of Justice Statistics. http://www.ojp.usdoj.gov/bjs/cvict_v.htm.

Walker, Samuel, Cassia Spohn, and Miriam DeLone. 1996. *The Color of Justice.* Belmont, CA: Wadsworth.

Wolfe, Timothy. 1996. "It's Not So Much the Armament that Is Frightening as It Is Their Willingness to Pull the Trigger: A Study of Juveniles' Deadly Fascination with Guns." Paper presented at the annual meeting of the Mid-South Sociological Association. Little Rock, AR, October.

Wolfgang, Marvin, Robert Figlio, and Thorsten Sellin. 1972. *Delinquency in a Birth Cohort.* Chicago: University of Chicago Press.

6

Agencies and Organizations

In this chapter, we list agencies and organizations that deal with the welfare of young people and their families, delinquent behavior, and juvenile justice. We have selected those agencies and organizations that have a proven track record; that is, they are known to be reputable and reliable. As you continue your research on juvenile delinquency, juvenile justice, and related topics, we hope that you find the information in this chapter as well as the next to be useful.

There are tens of thousands of agencies and organizations in the United States and abroad that deal with juvenile delinquency and juvenile justice; what we present in this chapter is only an introduction to what is out there. In an effort to bring some order to the vast array of such agencies and organizations, we have divided them into the following categories: child welfare and advocacy (including groups that work primarily to improve child care, family life, and education), delinquency prevention and treatment programs, and juvenile justice. We provide as much contact information as possible, including the most current Web site addresses (which are subject to change, sometimes quickly and often) and toll-free phone numbers (when available).

Child Welfare and Advocacy

There are a large number of agencies and organizations devoted to improving the lives of youngsters and their families. These organizations work directly with families in some cases, others are more policy oriented, while still others serve as resources for professionals and practitioners. The following list contains some of the most prominent and important of such groups.

Action Alliance for Children
1201 Martin Luther King Jr. Way
Oakland, CA 94612
Phone: 510-444-7136
Internet: http://www.4children.org

The Action Alliance for Children provides information on current problems, trends, and policies that affect children and their families. This is a great resource for policy makers, service providers, advocates, and the media. This organization also produces an award-winning magazine, *Children's Advocate*, and offers trainings and conferences.

Child Welfare League of America (CWLA)
440 First St. NW, 3rd Floor
Washington, DC 20001-2085
Phone: 202-638-2952
Internet: http://www.cwla.org/

CWLA is the oldest and largest nonprofit organization addressing issues of child welfare and family well-being at the national level. The organization has more than 1,000 private and public nonprofit agency members who work with children and families.

Children Now
1212 Broadway, 5th Floor
Oakland, CA 94612
Phone: 510-763-2444
Internet: http://www.childrennow.org

Children Now is an independent bipartisan organization that has been recognized for using the media to make positive changes. This organization also supports programs and research that deal with health insurance, positive media, early education, and after-school activities for children and working parents.

Children's Advocacy Institute
University of San Diego Law School
5998 Alcala Park
San Diego, CA 92110

Phone: 619-260-4806
Internet: http://www.caichildlaw.org

The Children's Advocacy Institute was founded in 1989 and is part of the Center for Public Interest Law at the University of San Diego. The institute advocates on the behalf of children through public education programs, in the court system, and in front of state legislatures. This organization also trains law students to work with children as advocates.

Children's Defense Fund (CDF)
25 E St. NW
Washington, DC 20001
Phone: 202-628-8787
Internet: http://www.childrensdefense.org

CDF and its committed staff have been advocates for the welfare of the country's children since 1973. This private nonprofit group focuses its efforts on shaping social policy so that "no child is left behind."

Children's Rights, Inc.
404 Park Ave. South, 11th Floor
New York, NY 10016
Phone: 212-683-2210
Internet: http://www.childrensrights

Children's Rights was part of the American Civil Liberties Union until 1995, when it became an independent nonprofit organization. This organization focuses on policy analysis to promote change in order to improve the child welfare system. Children's Rights also educates the public, advocates, and professionals about the child welfare system.

Eisenhower National Clearinghouse (ENC)
1929 Kenny Rd.
Columbus, OH 43210
Phone: 800-621-5785
Internet: http://www.enc.

The ENC, located on the campus of Ohio State University, is dedicated to the identification of effective educational programs, particularly those that help improve math and science teaching and learning for students K–12. The ENC maintains an excellent Web site that is filled with useful information.

Head Start
Internet: http://www2.acf.dhhs.gov/programs/hsb/

Head Start and Early Head Start are comprehensive child development programs serving the needs of children from birth to age five, pregnant women, and their families. All Head Start and Early Start programs are focused on the child. Their overall goal is to increase the school readiness of young children in low-income families. Head Start has been shown to be effective in improving school performance and reducing juvenile delinquency.

Kids Count: A Project of the Annie E. Casey Foundation
701 Saint Paul St.
Baltimore, MD 21202
Phone: 410-547-6600
Internet: http://www.aecf.org/kidscount/

Kids Count is a project of the Annie E. Casey Foundation. It provides a national and state-by-state tracking of the status of children in the United States. By providing policy makers and citizens with benchmarks of child well-being, Kids Count seeks to enrich local, state, and national discussions concerning ways to secure better futures for all children. Each year, Kids Count produces a national report that serves as a report card on how well children are faring in the United States.

National Association for the Education of Young Children (NAEYC)
1509 16th Street NW
Washington, DC 20036
E-mail: pubaff@naeyc.org

NAEYC is devoted to improving early childhood educational programs for children from birth through age eight. This is the largest organization of its kind and is well respected by professionals who work with young children.

National Association of Child Advocates (NACA)
1522 K Street NW, Suite 600
Washington, DC 20005-1202

Phone: 202-289-0776
Internet: http://www.childadvocacy.org

The mission of NACA is to improve the lives of children in the United States by enhancing the capacity of NACA member organizations to effectively advocate on behalf of children and their families. More than sixty agencies and organizations, at the state and national level, are members of this important association.

National Association for Multicultural Education
733 15th St. NW, Suite 430
Washington, DC 20005
Phone: 202-628-6263
Internet: http://www.nameorg.org

The National Association for Multicultural Education promotes social justice in education by providing multicultural education to all levels of education. This organization is supported by members, and it holds conferences and provides resources on multicultural education.

National Children's Advocacy Center
210 Pratt Ave.
Huntsville, AL 35801
Phone: 256-533-5437
Internet: http://www.nationalcac.org

The National Children's Advocacy Center is a nonprofit organization that provides services to abused children and their families. These services are provided through a multidisciplinary team who work together in order to reduce trauma for children. The first program began in 1985 in Huntsville, Alabama; there are now 400 programs nationwide.

National Coalition for Child Protection Reform
53 Skyhill Rd., Suite 202
Alexandria, VA 22314
Phone: 703-212-2006
Internet: http://www.nccpr.org

The National Coalition for Child Protection Reform works to improve policies on child abuse, foster care, and family preservation. This organization also provides information to the public, advocates, and professionals regarding child welfare.

Northwestern University/University of Chicago
Joint Center for Poverty Research (JCPR)
Northwestern University
2046 Sheridan Rd.
Evanston, IL 60208
Phone: 847-491-4145
Internet: http://www.jcpr.org

JCPR's mission is to advance the understanding of the causes and consequences of poverty in the United States. By using social science research, JCPR hopes to influence the discussion and formation of social policy. While it looks at poverty in general, it also looks at the ways poverty affects family functioning and the well-being of children.

Parent Help U.S.A.
330 W. Bay St., Suite 120
Costa Mesa, CA 92927
Phone: 949-650-3461
Internet: http://www.parenthelpusa.org

This nonprofit organization was started by Mothers and Others Against Child Abuse, Inc. Parent Help U.S.A. attempts to break the cycle of abuse by working with parents and children to provide parent education, counseling, and family services and promoting nonabusive ways to discipline.

Schott Center
678 Massachusetts Ave., Suite 301
Cambridge, MA 02139
Phone: 617-876-7700
Internet: http://www.schottfoundation.org

The Schott Center is part of the Caroline and Sigmund Schott Foundation, which funds programs that support equity in education and child care. In particular, the center funds programs that educate the public and policy makers on issues of early education, child care, and gender equity in education.

Stand Up for Kids
1510 Front St., Suite 100
San Diego, CA 92101

Phone: 800-365-4KID
Internet: http://www.50ways.org/ways/stand_up.html

Stand Up for Kids is a nonprofit volunteer organization dedicated to helping homeless and at-risk youth. The program started in 1990 and targets children under the age of twenty-one. There are now thirty outreach programs in fifteen states.

Youth Law Center
Children's Legal Protection Center
1010 Vermont Avenue NW, Suite 310
Washington, DC 20005-4902
Phone: 202-637-0377
E-mail: infor@youthlawcenter.com

The Youth Law Center is a nonprofit public-interest law firm that has worked to protect abused and at-risk children since 1978. With offices in San Francisco and Washington, D.C., the center works nationally to serve children, focusing particularly on the problems of children living apart from their families in child welfare and juvenile justice systems. The goal of the center's work is to ensure that vulnerable children are provided with the conditions and services they need to grow into healthy, productive adults.

Delinquency Prevention and Treatment

In this section, we list some of the most respected delinquency prevention and treatment agencies and organizations. As you will see below, some of these organizations are geared primarily toward research, while others are dedicated to providing treatment programming to youth and families.

Center for the Prevention of School Violence (CPSV)
Internet: http://www.ncdjjdp.org/cpsv/

The CPSV was established in 1993 as one of the first think tanks in the United States dedicated to preventing violence in schools. The center is part of the North Carolina Department of Juvenile Justice and Delinquency Prevention. Its Web site is filled with useful information on promoting safer and healthier schools. A special feature is a question-and-answer forum.

Center for the Study and Prevention of Violence
Institute of Behavioral Science
University of Colorado at Boulder
439 UCB
Boulder, CO 80309-0439
Phone: 303-492-8465
Internet: http://www.colorado.edu/cspv/

This research center is housed at the University of Colorado and is directed by one of the most respected researchers in the field of juvenile delinquency, Delbert Elliott. The center has done extensive research into which kinds of programs work to prevent youth violence.

Choice Program
The Shriver Center – UMBC
1000 Hilltop Circle
Baltimore, MD 21250
Phone: 410-455-2493
Internet: http://www.choiceprograms.org

The Choice Program is administered by the Shriver Center at the University of Maryland Baltimore County (UMBC). The program is aimed at reducing delinquent behavior before juveniles reach the point of no return (i.e., before they become so deeply enmeshed in a delinquent or criminal lifestyle that future options are effectively closed off). Youth in the program receive intensive supervision and mentoring from a well-trained case worker. A variety of issues—ranging from school performance to making wise choices—are addressed. In addition, young people in the program are provided with encouragement and support while still being held accountable for their actions.

Fast Track Project
Internet: http://www.fasttrackproject.org

The Fast Track Project is a multisite (with branches at Duke University, Penn State, University of Washington, and Vanderbilt University) intervention program that works with high-risk youth (identified as such as early as kindergarten). Recognizing that delinquent behavior is the result of multiple causes, this program seeks to address such causes comprehensively. The early findings suggest that this is a very promising approach to preventing and reducing delinquency, especially among the highest-risk population of youngster.

International Child and Youth Care Network
Internet: http://www.cyc-net.org

The International Child and Youth Care Network is an international nonprofit organization dedicated to informing child advocates. This site offers many resources, including an on-line magazine, journal articles, and chat rooms specifically designed to answer questions of advocates and professionals. This organization also holds conferences to further disseminate information regarding problems youth face internationally.

Juvenile Justice Clearinghouse
P.O. Box 6000
Rockville, MD 20849-6000
Phone: 800-638-8736

The mission of the OJJDP is to provide national leadership, coordination, and resources to prevent and respond to juvenile delinquency and victimization. OJJDP accomplishes this by supporting states and local communities in their efforts to develop and implement effective and coordinated prevention and intervention programs. OJJDP also helps these communities improve the juvenile justice system so that it protects the public safety, holds offenders accountable, and provides treatment and rehabilitative services tailored to the needs of families and the individual juvenile. OJJDP is one of the most important sources of funding and information on the prevention and treatment of delinquent behavior. They also maintain a clearinghouse that is an excellent resource for those working in the juvenile justice field. The clearinghouse consists of juvenile justice professionals who are available to answer questions, perform literature searches, and provide technical assistance for on-line materials. The clearinghouse also helps to distribute juvenile justice publications from OJJDP on their Web site and at conferences.

Multisystemic Therapy Services
Dr. Scott W. Henggeler
Family Services Research Center
Department of Psychiatry and Behavioral Sciences
Medical University of South Carolina

171 Ashley Ave.
Charleston, SC 29425-0742
Phone: 843-876-1800
Internet: http://www.mstservices.com

Multisystemic Therapy (MST) Services is a company that provides training and dissemination of information on one of the most effective treatment programs for serious and violent delinquent behavior. Based upon the recognition that delinquent behavior often reflects family problems as well as a multitude of other difficulties, MST provides intensive therapy that addresses all of these issues. To date, the evaluation studies of MST have been very positive.

National Academies
500 Fifth St. NW
Washington, DC 20001
Internet: http://www.nationalacademies.org

The National Academies brings together scientists from a variety of areas of expertise. These experts volunteer by advising the public and government about public policy. The National Academies has recently formed a panel to address juvenile crime focusing on prevention, treatment, and control.

National Council on Alcoholism and Drug Dependence (NCADD)
20 Exchange Place, Suite 2902
New York, NY 10005
Phone: 212-269-7797
Hope Line (24-hour Affiliate Referral): 800-NCA-CALL
Internet: http://www.ncadd.org

The NCADD was founded in 1944 by Marty Mann, the first woman to find long-term sobriety through the help of Alcoholics Anonymous (AA). The NCADD advocates prevention, intervention, and treatment of alcoholism and other drug addictions. Efforts to reduce and prevent drug abuse should help also reduce and prevent delinquent behavior. The NCADD has offices in New York and Washington, D.C., as well as a nationwide network of affiliates.

**National Council on Crime and Delinquency
(Headquarters)**
1970 Broadway, Suite 500
Oakland, CA 94612
Phone: 510-208-0500
Fax: 510-208-0511

**National Council on Crime and Delinquency
(Midwest Office)**
426 S. Yellowstone Dr., Suite 250
Madison, WI 53719
Phone: 608-831-8882
Fax: 608-831-6446
E-mail: Anne Boldon at aboldon@mw.nccd-crc.org
Internet: http://www.nccd-crc.org

The National Council on Crime and Delinquency (NCCD) is a
nonprofit organization founded in 1907. Its mission is to work toward improving the juvenile justice system for all youth. The
NCCD works with juvenile justice agencies at the state and national levels to evaluate ongoing programs, provide comprehensive analyses for future programs and initiatives, and provide detailed planning for correctional needs, for both juveniles and
adults, as well as for the prevention of youth violence. The
NCCD also works with child service and juvenile justice agencies
to prevent child abuse. Associated with the NCCD is the Children's Research Center (CRC).

National Mentoring Partnership
1600 Duke St., Suite 300
Alexandria, VA 22314
Phone: 703-224-2200
Internet: http://www.mentoring.org

In 1990, philanthropists started the National Mentoring Partnership with the intent of spreading mentor programs across the
country. This organization has noticed that there are barriers to
implementing mentoring programs nationwide, and its members
educate both the public and mentoring programs about identifying these barriers and successfully moving past them.

National Network for Youth
1319 F St. NW, Suite 401

Washington, DC 20004-1106
Phone: 202-783-7949
Internet: http://www.nn4youth.org

The National Network for Youth is a nonprofit organization that supports 800 community-based organizations for youth nationwide. This organization provides information and technical assistance to community programs so that these programs can be more effective. The network also helps educate the public and influence policy regarding youth.

National Youth Violence Prevention Resource Center (NYVPRC)
Internet: http://www.safeyouth.org

The NYVPRC is the result of collaboration between the Centers for Disease Control and other federal agencies. The center serves as a single point of access to federal information on youth violence prevention and suicide. It maintains a Web site that is easy to navigate and filled with useful information.

Office of Juvenile Justice and Delinquency Prevention (OJJDP)
810 Seventh St. NW
Washington, DC 20531
Phone: 202-307-5911
Internet: http://www.ojjdp.ncjrs.org

Oregon Social Learning Center (OSLC)
160 E. Fourth Ave.
Eugene, OR 97401
Phone: 541-485-2711
Internet: http://www.oslc.org

The Oregon Social Learning Center (OSLC) is a nonprofit and independent research center committed to increasing the understanding of the social and psychological factors that influence parenting and family functioning. The center's staff members are some of the foremost authorities on the relationship between family life and juvenile delinquency. The center has developed and implemented a number of successful parenting programs that prevent and reduce delinquent behavior. This program is also discussed in Chapter 2.

The Perry Preschool Program
High Scope Educational Research Foundation
600 N. River St.
Ypsilanti, MI 48198-2898
Phone: 734-485-2000
Internet: http://www.highscope.org/Research/PerryProject/
perrymain.htm

The Perry Preschool Program, sponsored by the High Scope Educational Research Foundation, is one of the most well-known examples of a successful delinquency prevention program. A study of 123 low-income African American youth was conducted to see what effects, if any, would result from a high-quality preschool program. The youth were randomly put into either the experimental group (i.e., those who received the preschool program) or the control group (i.e., those who received no preschool programming). The study provided overwhelming data that those youth who took part in the preschool program were much less likely to be involved in delinquent behavior. Even as adults, those youth who went to the preschool program did much better in terms of income, home ownership, commitment to marriage, and social responsibility. This program is also discussed in Chapter 2.

Strengthening America's Families
University of Utah
Phone: 801-581-8498
Internet: http://www.strengtheningfamilies.org

In 1999, the Office of Juvenile Justice and Delinquency Prevention assessed which family programs for delinquency prevention were effective. This Web site provides a literature review for effective programming and also detailed information on each of the programs.

Youth Villages
Stacy Porter, Staff Recruiter
3915 Bristol Highway, Suite 202
Johnson City, TN 37601
Phone: 423-283-6513
Fax: 423-283-6550
E-mail: stacy.porter@youthvillages.org
Internet: http://www.youthvillages.org

Youth Villages is a private, not-for-profit organization with services offered in five states, particularly in Tennessee and Mississippi. The purpose of Youth Villages is to work with troubled youth and their families in an effort to prevent and reduce juvenile delinquency. The program's philosophy is to provide a variety of services to youth and their families, including residential treatment services, home counseling, and crisis assistance. With a staff of over 1,000, Youth Villages is able to work with a variety of cases and for various periods of time. A recent treatment programs is Intensive In-Home Family Treatment, which uses multisystemic therapy (MST) as an important component of its treatment philosophy.

Juvenile Justice

In this final section of the chapter, we provide a list of agencies and organizations that are involved in promoting a fair and effective juvenile justice system. Some of these organizations are geared primarily toward professionals and practitioners, while others are dedicated to shaping juvenile justice policy.

Administration for Children and Families
National Clearinghouse on Families and Youth
P.O. Box 13505
Silver Springs, MD 20911-3505
Phone: 301-608-8098
Internet: http://www.acf.hhs.gov/

The Administration for Children and Families is funded by the U.S. Department of Health and Human Services. This organization oversees federal programs that work with children, families, and communities to improve their environment and well-being. The Web site has a list of publications for juvenile justice professionals that was put together by the National Clearinghouse on Families and Youth.

American Bar Association (ABA) Juvenile Justice Center
740 15th Street NW, 10th Floor
Washington, DC 20005
Phone: 202-662-1506
Internet: http://www.abanet.org/crimjust/juvjus/

The ABA is a voluntary association of lawyers dedicated to improving the nation's legal system. The Juvenile Justice Center of the ABA focuses its attention on the state of the U.S. juvenile justice system.

American Youth Policy Forum (AYPF)
Internet: http://www.aypf.org

The AYPF is a nonprofit and nonpartisan organization dedicated to providing learning opportunities for policy makers on matters of social policy that affect children. Its work is aimed at the national, state, and local levels.

Building Blocks for Youth
Internet: http://www.buildingblocksforyouth.org

Building Blocks for Youth is an alliance of children's advocates, researchers, law enforcement professionals, and community organizers that seeks to protect minority youth in the juvenile justice system and promote rational and effective justice policies.

Bureau of Justice Assistance (BJA)
810 Seventh St. NW, 4th Floor
Washington, DC 20531
Phone: 202-616-6500
Internet: http://www.ojp.usdoj.gov/BJA/

The BJA is an arm of the Office of Justice Programs, Department of Justice. BJA is dedicated to improving the juvenile and criminal justice systems. It provides support and assistance to communities and professionals in a wide variety of ways and maintains an excellent Web site.

Center for Effective Collaboration and Practice
1000 Thomas Jefferson St. NW, Suite 400
Washington, DC 20007
Phone: 202-944-5400
Internet: http://www.air.org/cecp/

Funded by the U.S. Department of Education's Office of Special Education Programs, the center was developed to help children with emotional and behavioral problems in order to prevent future delinquency problems. The center accomplishes this mission by identifying programs that work for children with emotional and behavioral problems and then promoting these programs to policy makers and the public.

Center on Juvenile and Criminal Justice
1234 Massachusetts Ave NW, Suite C1009
Washington, DC 20005
Phone: 202-737-7270
Internet: http://www.cjcj.org

The Center on Juvenile and Criminal Justice is committed to finding alternatives to incarceration as a solution to the problem of juvenile delinquency. The center provides assistance to local and state governments that are looking for alternatives to the incarceration of juveniles.

Coalition for Juvenile Justice (CJJ)
Internet: http://www.juvjustice.org

CJJ is a national group of professionals and others interested in the well-being of youth, families, and communities. It promotes sensible and sensitive juvenile justice programs and policies.

Justice Policy Institute
4455 Connecticut Ave NW, Suite B-500
Washington, DC 20008
Phone: 202-363-7847
Internet: http://www.justicepolicy.org

The Justice Policy Institute is a think tank that attempts to reduce the overreliance of our criminal justice system on incarceration. This organization's goal is to find new solutions to solve this problem. This think tank focuses on public policy regarding juvenile justice reform and educating the public.

Juvenile Justice Evaluation Center (JJEC)
Internet: http://www.jrsa.org/jjec/

The JJEC maintains a Web site that disseminates information to practitioners on the effectiveness of various juvenile justice programs. The Web site provides a wealth of useful information on current juvenile justice initiatives and efforts.

Kids Counsel: Center for Children's Advocacy
University of Connecticut School of Law

65 Elizabeth St.
Hartford, CT 06105
Internet: http://www.kidscounsel.org/kidscounsel/

Kids Counsel is an organization based at the University of Connecticut's Law School. This organization is useful for professionals working with children who are involved in the juvenile justice system. The Web site covers recent state and federal legislation passed concerning children as well as other legal resources such as documents and links. This organization also has training seminars for professionals.

National Association of Counsel for Children
1825 Marion St., Suite 340
Denver, CO 80218
Phone: 888-828-NACC
Internet: http://www.naccchildlaw.org

The National Association of Counsel for Children was founded in 1977 as a nonprofit child advocacy and professional organization. This organization trains attorneys and other professionals working with children. It also provides information about child advocacy to the public and shapes public policy and legislation concerning children.

National Council of Juvenile and Family Court Judges (NCJFCJ)
Internet: http://www.ncjfcj.org

NCJFCJ is committed to improving the lives of children and families by reforming and improving family and juvenile courts across the United States. Its members, as its name indicates, are judges who preside over courts of juvenile and family jurisdiction.

Office of Juvenile Justice and Delinquency Prevention (OJJDP)
Internet: http://www.ojjdp.ncjrs.org

OJJDP is the largest and perhaps most important federal agency addressing the problems of juvenile delinquency and juvenile justice (for more information, see the entry on OJJDP in the section on Delinquency Prevention and Treatment). OJJDP maintains a Web site that is an excellent place to begin research into juvenile justice.

The Sentencing Project
Internet: http://www.sentencingproject.org

The Sentencing Project is widely recognized as a national leader in research and advocacy for alternative criminal and juvenile justice policy. Many of the project's reports have been used to demonstrate the racial disparity that plagues the U.S. criminal justice system. The organization maintains a Web site that is a good source of information on crime, delinquency, and justice in the United States.

In this chapter, we have listed some of the most important and respected agencies and organizations dealing with child welfare, delinquency prevention and treatment, and juvenile justice. In the next chapter, we will provide other sources of information—both print and nonprint—that will aid in the research of juvenile justice and delinquent behavior. A key to learning as much as you can about these topics is to maintain a curious and open mind.

7

Selected Print and Nonprint Resources

I n this chapter, we list some of the most important and respected sources of information on delinquency and juvenile justice. The first section lists books, periodicals, and other printed sources of information on delinquency. These sources are grouped by subject.

The nonprint sources of information are listed in the second section. The Internet Web sites are accurate as of the time of printing, but we must caution readers that Web sites appear, change addresses, and disappear with great frequency. Films relating to juvenile delinquency and the juvenile justice system also are listed.

Print Sources

General/Introductory Books on Juvenile Delinquency

Agnew, Robert. 2001. *Juvenile Delinquency: Causes and Control.* Los Angeles: Roxbury.

This book is 392 pages long. Agnew examines the antecedents to juvenile delinquency and society's reaction, along with the legal system's attempt to solve the problems related to juvenile crime. This text addresses three major questions: What is the nature and extent of juvenile delinquency? What are the causes of juvenile delinquency? And how can we best control delinquency? Agnew presents the theories of strain, social learning, and control in an easy-to-understand manner while elaborating on how these theories have influenced the field of juvenile delinquency in both theory and research. For those just beginning in the field of juvenile delinquency, this book is easy to read and understand.

Bartollas, Clemens. 2003. *Juvenile Delinquency,* 6th ed. New York: Allyn and Bacon.

This book is 576 pages long. A special feature is its emphasis on propositions that are summarized at the end of the book. Bartollas offers many insights into the nature of delinquency from a sociological perspective. This book is broken down into five main sections that cover the nature and extent of delinquency; causes of delinquency; environmental influences on delinquents; prevention, diversion, and treatment; and the social control of delinquency. This text also includes the social contexts of delinquency, social policy and policy recommendations, and examples of real delinquent cases for a better understanding of how a delinquent is treated within the juvenile system.

Bartollas, Clemens, ed. 2003. *Voices of Delinquency.* New York: Allyn and Bacon.

This is a brief book, 102 pages long, but it is full of firsthand accounts of why adult criminals started on a path of crime and delinquency and, ultimately, encountered long prison terms or the death penalty. The "stories," as Bartollas calls them, are recollections from prison inmates interviewed by or known to the author. Many of these inmates have been convicted of murder or other violent crimes. Bartollas does an excellent job of both capturing the thoughts and perspectives of these inmates and reporting their life histories and their journeys into crime and delinquency. The identities of the inmates are known only to the author, although some inmates chose to reveal their true names. However, their stories are very real. This book is highly recommended for those interested in explanations of crime and delinquency given by the offenders themselves, as opposed to the thoughts and reflections of others.

Bynum, Jack E., and William E. Thompson. 2005. *Juvenile Delinquency: A Sociological Approach,* 6th ed. Boston: Allyn and Bacon.

This book, 560 pages long, looks at the issue of juvenile delinquency by combining information from the disciplines of sociology, criminology, and social work. In particular, the text focuses on delinquency and how a youth's family, neighborhood, school, peer group, and social class affect his/her behavior. This volume is enriched with contributions from those who work in the field of juvenile delinquency, such as psychologists and social workers, and is supplemented with cross-cultural comparisons of juvenile delinquency and current controversial topics in the field. This text is divided into six main sections: conformity, deviance, and juvenile delinquency; causes of juvenile delinquency; juvenile delinquency in a social context; social control; the juvenile justice system; and strategies for dealing with juvenile delinquency.

Chesney-Lind, Meda, and Randall G. Shelden. 2003. *Girls, Delinquency, and Juvenile Justice,* 3rd ed. Belmont, CA: Wadsworth.

This book is 345 pages in length. The authors examine the issues of female juvenile delinquency and theories that apply to female juvenile delinquents, along with the life experiences of female delinquents, which generally include previous abuse. This book features chapters on topics such as girls and gangs, how girls are treated in the juvenile justice system both currently and historically, and girls in detention. The text also examines gender differences throughout the juvenile justice system. This is a timely book, because delinquent girls are often a forgotten segment of the juvenile justice system.

Kratcoski, Peter C., and Lucille Dunn Kratcoski. 2004. *Juvenile Delinquency,* 5th ed. Upper Saddle River, NJ: Prentice-Hall.

This book is 480 pages in length. Juvenile delinquency is examined from a sociological approach and takes into consideration environmental influences. This volume examines contemporary society's effect on delinquent behavior, as well as its response to delinquent acts. Features include a focus on emotional, physical, and sexual abuse of children and the effect of abuse on delinquency. Recent court cases regarding juveniles are also examined.

Laub, John H., and Robert J. Sampson. 2003. *Shared Beginnings, Divergent Lives: Delinquent Boys to Age 70*. Boston: Harvard University Press.

This book is 352 pages long. The authors examine recently collected data stemming from Sheldon and Eleanor Gleuck's 1950 study of 500 boys in Boston who had been sent to a reformatory school. The boys, now men in their seventies, offer insight into how some remained engaged in criminal activities, while others did not.

Lotz, Roy. 2005. *Youth Crime in America: A Modern Synthesis*. Upper Saddle River, NJ: Pearson/Prentice-Hall.

This book offers a general overview of juvenile crime in the United States. The book is 337 pages long and contains twelve chapters. The topics covered in this volume range from statistical information on delinquency to punishment and control of juvenile crime. There are good discussions of major theoretical explanations of crime, including individualistic and sociological theories. There are also discussions of institutional contexts of delinquency, especially the family and the school. The author covers peer associations as an important contributory context for delinquency, but he does not consider the separate influence of juvenile gangs.

Muncie, John. 2004. *Youth and Crime*. Thousand Oaks, CA: Sage.

This book is 384 pages in length. The author pulls together information from multiple disciplines to examine juvenile crime, the justice system, and the evolution of both. This text begins with data on youth crime and the history of juvenile delinquency. The author then focuses on theoretical explanations of juvenile crime, and the last part of this text examines contemporary juvenile delinquency, cultural issues, and the compromises and contradictions of the juvenile system today.

Samenow, Stanton E. 2001. *Before It's Too Late: Why Some Kids Get into Trouble and What Parents Can Do About It*. New York: Crown.

This book is 240 pages in length. Samenow is a psychologist who focuses upon the issues of antisocial children and gives practical advice for parents and practitioners on how to work with these at-risk youth. This book focuses on identifying phases versus serious delinquent behavior and provides information on antisocial behavior in children and how parents can take action if necessary.

Shoemaker, Donald J. 2005. *Theories of Delinquency: An Examination of Explanations of Delinquent Behavior,* 5th ed. New York: Oxford University Press.

This is an overview of important theoretical explanations of delinquency. The book is 310 pages long and is composed of twelve chapters. Each chapter concerns a particular explanation of delinquency; there is a special chapter on female crime and delinquency. The last chapter is a discussion of theory integration and its logic, structure, and utility. The book is primarily intended for upper-level college courses, including graduate courses, but it is also useful for general audiences.

Siegel, Larry J. 2001. *Juvenile Delinquency: The Core.* Belmont, CA: Wadsworth.

This book is 416 pages in length. Siegel examines theory and policy regarding juvenile justice from the early 1900s to the present day. This book is divided into four sections: background information in delinquency and related theories, preventing delinquency in early childhood, preventing delinquency in the family and community, and new directions in preventing delinquency through tertiary prevention efforts.

Siegel, Larry J., Brandon C. Walsh, and Joseph J. Senna. 2002. *Juvenile Delinquency: Theory, Practice, and Law,* 8th ed. Belmont, CA: Wadsworth.

This book is 592 pages in length. This text covers theory, juvenile delinquency, and policy, using up-to-date research and policy examples to help the reader obtain a better grasp of current issues. Features of this text include a comprehensive review of the literature and current news. Controversial aspects of juvenile delinquency are examined in an unbiased manner.

Trojanowicz, Robert C., Merry Morash, and Pamela J. Schram. 2001. *Juvenile Delinquency: Concepts and Control,* 6th ed. Upper Saddle River, NJ: Prentice-Hall.

This book is 461 pages long and provides an overview of juvenile delinquency, including theories, prevention, and policies. Issues that children face, such as peer pressure and victimization, and their impact on juvenile delinquency are also discussed. The authors discuss minorities, lower-class youth, and their vulnerabilities within the juvenile justice system, as well as the process that juveniles go through from contact with the arresting officer to detention or treatment.

Weisheit, Ralph A., and Robert G. Culbertson, eds. 1999. *Juvenile Delinquency: A Justice Perspective,* 4th ed. Long Grove, IL: Waveland.

This book is 318 pages in length. The authors examine responses to juvenile crime, as well as important topics such as school violence, restorative justice, and the effect of childhood trauma on delinquency. This text is divided into five main sections: the delinquency problem and the justice system, sources of delinquency, juveniles in the system, juveniles in confinement, and policy considerations.

History of Juvenile Delinquency and Juvenile Justice

Binder, Arnold, Gilbert Geis, and Dickson D. Bruce, Jr. 2001. *Juvenile Delinquency: Historical, Cultural, and Legal Perspectives,* 3rd ed. Cincinnati, OH: Anderson.

This book is 517 pages in length. The authors take a historical look at theories, policies, and public opinion regarding the juvenile justice system. This book is interdisciplinary in nature and reviews theories on juvenile delinquency from both psychological and sociological perspectives. The authors examine community-based programs for youthful offenders and offer examples of successful programs.

Cox, Pamela, and Heather Shore, eds. 2002. *Becoming Delinquent: British and European Youth, 1650-1950.* Aldershot, United Kingdom: Ashgate.

This book, 200 pages long, provides an overview of juvenile delinquency in western Europe over the past three centuries, as well as how the concept of juvenile justice has been shaped by moral panics.

Feld, Barry C. 1999. *Bad Kids: Race and the Transformation of the Juvenile Court.* Oxford: Oxford University Press.

This book is 392 pages in length. The author examines the changes in the juvenile court over the past three decades and how the court used to focus upon rehabilitation and now is concerned with punishment. The social and legal implications that spurred these changes also are examined.

Fishman, Sarah. 2002. *Battle for Children.* Boston: Harvard University Press.

This book is 320 pages in length. Fishman focuses upon World War II and how the war changed the juvenile justice system in France from a punitive system to a treatment-oriented one. The author looks at how the war caused juvenile delinquency in France to increase in response to poverty and not family dislocation.

Knupher, Anne Meis. 2001. *Reform and Resistance: Gender, Delinquency and America's First Juvenile Court.* London: Routledge.

This book is 304 pages in length. The author examines what it meant to be a delinquent female in the late nineteenth and early twentieth centuries, how these young girls were treated, and how gender affected the first juvenile court systems.

Platt, Anthony M. 1977. *The Child Savers: The Invention of Delinquency,* 2nd ed., enlarged. Chicago: University of Chicago Press.

This book, 230 pages in length, is considered a classic in the field. Platt provides a good overview of the historical movement to create the modern juvenile justice system. He identifies many of the important historical events in this development. An important feature of this book is the detailed discussions provided on the people involved in the juvenile justice movement, especially in the nineteenth century. Platt refers to these individuals as "child savers" and their efforts as the "child-saving movement." However, he also discusses the motives of these child savers in critical terms. That is, he challenges the purity of the motives of the child savers and argues that many of them wanted to preserve middle-class values and lifestyles in creating the juvenile justice system as we know it today.

Rosenheim, Margaret K., Franklin E. Zimring, David S. Tanenhaus, and Bernardine Dohrn, eds. 2002. *A Century of Juvenile Justice.* Chicago: University of Chicago Press.

This is a 554-page collection of original articles on the juvenile justice system in the United States, from its origins in the early nineteenth century to contemporary times. Besides being an excellent source for the historical roots of the modern system of juvenile justice, this book provides interesting analyses on many contemporary issues, such as the changing conceptions of status offenders and issues affecting contemporary juvenile courts in the United States. The final section of the book provides information on systems of juvenile justice in other countries, such as England, Scotland, Wales, and Japan.

Sharp, Paul M., and Barry W. Hancock. 1998. *Juvenile Delinquency: Historical, Theoretical and Societal Reactions to Youth,* 2nd ed. Upper Saddle River, NJ: Prentice-Hall.

The authors have put together current and classic articles in this 436-page book, which examines the history and theory behind juvenile delinquency as well as society's reaction to this issue. This book is divided into five main sections: historical, theoretical, societal, institutional, and public policy concerns. The text also discusses female delinquency and the impact of gender on legal issues and public policy.

Vito, Gennaro F., and Clifford E. Simonsen. 2004. *Juvenile Justice Today,* 4th ed. Upper Saddle River, NJ: Prentice-Hall.

This book is 400 pages in length and is an overview of the history and development of the juvenile justice system. This text focuses on the operation of the juvenile justice system and the employees who make it work, along with treatment programs aimed at youthful offenders. This book is divided into three main sections: the history of the juvenile justice system, the juvenile justice process, and the future of the juvenile justice system. This text also includes helpful Web sites to allow the reader to refer to up-to-date statistics.

Yablonsky, Lewis. 1999. *Juvenile Delinquency: Into the Twenty-First Century*. Belmont, CA: Wadsworth.

This book is 400 pages long. Yablonsky provides an overview of juvenile delinquency and the juvenile justice system over the past 100 years, along with thoughts on where the juvenile system is heading. This book is enriched with the author's experiences as a researcher working with children incarcerated in a psychiatric hospital.

General/Introductory Books on the Juvenile Justice System

Bartol, Curt R., and Anne M. Bartol. 1998. *Delinquency and Justice: A Psychosocial Approach*, 2nd ed. Upper Saddle River, NJ: Prentice-Hall.

This book is 387 pages in length. The authors discuss the causes, preventions, and interventions associated with juvenile delinquency from a developmental perspective. The authors divide juvenile delinquents into two categories: those who offend in response to social pressures and those who are life course offenders. Included in this book is a discussion of how psychological issues such as attention deficit disorder, antisocial behavior, and learning disorders affect juveniles and lead to delinquent behavior.

Bartollas, Clemens, and Stuart Miller. 2005. *Juvenile Justice in America*, 4th ed. Upper Saddle River, New Jersey: Pearson/Prentice-Hall.

In this 570-page volume, the authors focus upon juvenile justice theory and research both in the United States and internationally in countries such as England and Wales, Australia, Canada, China, South Africa, India, and Brazil. In addition, there are discussions of types of juvenile offenders and explanations of why juveniles commit crimes. The chapters on juvenile justice are thorough and well informed, and they address all of the major components of juvenile justice. The book closes with a good discussion of the future of juvenile justice and treatment programs for juvenile offenders in the United States.

Champion, Dean John. 2004. *The Juvenile Justice System: Delinquency, Processing and the Law,* 4th ed. Upper Saddle River, NJ: Prentice-Hall.

This book is 608 pages long. Champion provides an overview of the juvenile justice system from a legal perspective. This text focuses upon the nature of delinquency; how juvenile offenders are classified; and juvenile courts, juvenile corrections, and the rights of juvenile offenders.

Fagan, Jeffrey, and Franklin E. Zimring, eds. 2000. *Changing Borders of Juvenile Justice: Transfer of Adolescents to the Criminal Court.* Chicago: University of Chicago Press.

This book, 440 pages long, focuses on the issue of juvenile transfer and how there are more juveniles being transferred to adult court than ever before despite the decrease in violent crime rates among youth. This book analyzes the policy of juvenile transfer, how juvenile transfer came about, and what it means for the juvenile justice system.

Grisso, Thomas, and Robert G. Schwartz, eds. 2003. *Youth on Trial: A Developmental Perspective on Juvenile Justice.* Chicago: University of Chicago Press.

This book is 472 pages in length and examines the developmental process of adolescents. It applies this knowledge to juvenile transfer specifically and looks at whether juveniles are developmentally capable of understanding and handling the adult court system.

Hartjen, Clayton A., and S. Priyadarsini. 2004. *Delinquency and Justice: An International Bibliography.* Westport, CT: Praeger.

This volume offers an annotated collection of books, book chapters, and journal articles published between 1975 and 2001. In this bibliography there are over sixty countries represented, including the United States. This annotated bibliography is truly an ambitious project, and it addresses a number of issues related to current knowledge about juvenile delinquency and juvenile justice from a global perspective. It promises to be one of the most useful bibliographic resources published on this topic.

Houston, James, and Shannon M. Barton. 2005. *Juvenile Justice: Theory, Systems, and Organization.* Upper Saddle River, NJ: Pearson/Prentice-Hall.

Houston and Barton provide a useful introduction to the modern juvenile justice system in the United States. Their book, 382 pages long, examines juvenile justice concepts and current societal issues. The book considers most of the major players in the juvenile justice system, from the police and probation officers to juvenile court judges and correctional personnel. The authors also discuss important issues in the modern juvenile justice system, such as waivers to the criminal court and the death penalty for juvenile criminals. There are even chapters on delinquency causation and institutional factors, such as the family and the school. This book should be useful for the practitioner as well as the student of delinquency.

Howell, James C. 2003. *Preventing and Reducing Juvenile Delinquency: A Comprehensive Framework.* Thousand Oaks, CA: Sage.

This book is 416 pages in length. Howell discusses the strengths and weaknesses of the juvenile justice system. In particular, he focuses on how the system can be strengthened to improve counseling and rehabilitation programs for youthful offenders. Case studies are used throughout the book to better understand the juvenile justice system from an individual perspective. This text is divided into three main sections: the historical context of current juvenile justice systems policies and practices, research based on juvenile offenders and what does not work, and effective prevention and rehabilitation programs in a comprehensive framework.

Jackson, Mary S., and Paul Knepper. 2003. *Delinquency and Justice.* Boston: Allyn and Bacon.

This book is 448 pages in length and examines the juvenile court system, ethnicity, and gender. This book is an excellent study for anyone interested in working with juvenile offenders because of its coverage of issues, policies, and rationales of the juvenile court system.

Krisberg, Barry. 2004 *Juvenile Justice: Redeeming Our Children.* Thousand Oaks, CA: Sage.

This is a 240-page book that covers several issues concerning the contemporary juvenile justice system in the United States. The author traces the historical development of the U.S. juvenile justice system, as well as the development of houses of refuge, from their origins to contemporary times. Some of the current issues addressed in this book include racial and gender discrimination within the system, gang control problems and strategies, and effective treatment programs and strategies.

Krisberg, Barry, and James F. Austin. 1993. *Reinventing Juvenile Justice.* Thousand Oaks, CA: Sage.

This book is 222 pages in length. The authors discuss the current juvenile system, its problems, and possible solutions. The text focuses upon the history of juvenile justice in comparison to the contemporary juvenile justice system, taking into consideration the impact of race and gender. Projects such as the Massachusetts experiment are discussed as an example of what is successful in the juvenile system.

Mays, Larry G., and L. Thomas Winfree, Jr. 1999. *Juvenile Justice.* New York: McGraw-Hill.

This book, 432 pages in length, is written from a political science and sociological perspective. It focuses on the history of the juvenile justice system, current issues, and how a juvenile is processed through the system.

Parry, David L. 2004. *Essential Readings in Juvenile Justice.* Upper Saddle River, NJ: Pearson/Prentice-Hall.

This book contains fifty-seven articles placed in ten chapters over 414 pages. This volume is a useful resource for scholars and students of delinquency. Many of its articles have been cited in the literature. In addition, there is a separate chapter on important court decisions, early and modern, such as *Ex Parte Crouse*. An interesting feature of the book is the inclusion of important U.S. Supreme Court decisions. The inclusion of these decisions is especially useful because the author presents the cases and the issues in full detail.

Roberts, Albert A., ed. 2004. *Juvenile Justice Sourcebook: Past, Present, and Future.* New York: Oxford University Press.

This anthology offers original articles on important topics of juvenile justice in the United States with, as the title suggests, historical, contemporary, and even predictive assessments. The book totals 628 pages and is comprehensive in its coverage of important issues concerning U.S. juvenile justice. Topics covered in the twenty chapters include school violence, issues of treatment, detention, female delinquency, mental illness and delinquency, the death penalty for juveniles, and restorative justice. This is a useful resource for the professional as well as the layperson interested in a handy collection of informative articles.

Whitehead, John T., and Steven P. Lab. 2003. *Juvenile Justice: An Introduction,* 4th ed. Cincinnati, OH: Anderson.

This book is 480 pages in length. The authors examine the juvenile justice system, its policies, and theories. The authors look at issues within juvenile justice related to gender, youth gangs, and youth and the death penalty, along with correctional philosophies that have been applied to youthful offenders.

Williams, Frank P., and Marilyn D. McShane, eds. 2002. *Encyclopedia of Juvenile Justice.* Thousand Oaks, CA: Sage.

The editors of this encyclopedia, which is 416 pages long, have put together more than 200 articles on juvenile justice, ranging from substance abuse to society's reaction to the juvenile justice system. This encyclopedia covers a vast array of topics, but it is easy to use and understand because it is free of jargon. Entries are written by top researchers and practitioners within the juvenile justice field.

Periodicals That Focus on Juvenile Justice and Juvenile Delinquency

Crime and Delinquency

Sage

This journal is published quarterly and discusses policy and program analysis.

Crime Prevention and Community Safety: An International Journal

Perpetuity

This journal addresses crime prevention internationally, specifically examining the causes of crime and possible solutions. Topics covered range from the evaluation of crime prevention strategies to fear of crime.

Criminal Justice Ethics

Institute for Criminal Justice Ethics

This journal examines ethical concerns in the criminal justice system and attempts to draw ethical issues into the spotlight for both practitioners and the general public. This publication is semiannual and includes topics such as the decision to prosecute and punishment.

Deviant Behavior

Taylor and Francis

This is the only journal that focuses specifically on deviant behavior; in particular, on theories of deviance and research conducted on this topic. Articles address issues such as juvenile delinquency, substance abuse, and mental illness.

Journal of Adolescence

Elsevier

This bimonthly publication covers the topics of adolescent development, effective coping skills, treatment, and intervention.

Journal of Ethnicity in Criminal Justice
Hawthorn

This journal examines how race and ethnicity influence our criminal justice system. Articles cover important research, theory, and policy regarding ethnicity and the criminal justice system.

Journal of Gang Research
National Gang Research Center

This quarterly publication investigates research topics related to gangs and their members. This journal hopes to give practitioners and the public a better understanding of gangs in order to examine the problems associated with gangs and possible solutions.

Journal of Juvenile Justice
National Juvenile Detention Association

This journal is published quarterly and examines effective strategies for detention centers, the operation of juvenile facilities, trends, and legal issues.

Journal of Research in Crime and Delinquency
Sage

This journal is published quarterly and covers controversies and current issues in criminal justice. It takes a research-oriented, as opposed to a policy-oriented, approach in order to help explain and further the understanding of the issues.

Juvenile and Family Court Journal
National Council of Juvenile and Family Court Judges

This journal is published quarterly and discusses juvenile justice and family law. Once a year this journal dedicates an issue to a relevant special topic.

Reclaiming Children and Youth: Journal of Strength-Based Interventions
International Child and Youth Care Network

This journal is published quarterly and promotes a network of knowledge for those who work with children in the family, school, and community settings.

Women and Criminal Justice
Hawthorn

This journal provides information for practitioners and researchers wanting to better understand current issues in criminal justice that specifically affect women. Articles address research, theory, and policy and cover topics that range from women and the law to women working in the criminal justice field.

Youth Violence and Juvenile Justice
Sage

This journal is published quarterly and examines research, theory, and current policy in the area of youth violence, juvenile justice, and school safety.

Nonprint Sources

General Information on Juvenile Delinquency and Juvenile Justice

http://www.afterschool.gov

Web site providing information on **federal resources that support children and youth during out-of-school hours.**

Mailing Address:
Dr. Vicky Moss
1800 F St. NW, Room 7104
Washington, DC 20405
Phone: 202-208-1309
E-mail: afterschool@gsa.gov

http://www.abanet.org/crimjust/juvjus/

Web site of the **American Bar Association's Juvenile Justice Center.** Provides information on such important issues as juveniles and the death penalty, protecting juveniles' civil rights, and improving the juvenile justice system.

Mailing Address:
American Bar Association
541 N. Fairbanks Court

Chicago, IL 60611
Phone: 800-285-2221
Fax: 312-988-5528

http://www.buildingblocksforyouth.org

Web site for **Building Blocks for Youth**, which provides information on effective juvenile justice policies and links to current news
about juvenile justice.

E-mail: info.bby@erols.com

http://www.ojp.usdoj.gov/bjs

Web site for the **Bureau of Justice Statistics**. This site provides a
database where one can search for articles regarding statistics
and criminal justice.

Mailing Address:
810 Seventh St. NW
Washington, DC 20531
Phone: 202-307-0765
E-mail: askbjs@ojp.usdoj.gov

http://www.cjcj.org

Web site for the **Center on Juvenile and Criminal Justice**, which
provides a list of effective programs that serve as alternatives to
incarceration and information on how to implement these programs. The center helps train practitioners working with juveniles to provide more effective services. It also examines policy issues and is currently working on projects that address the issues
of gender, race, and juvenile justice.

Mailing Address:
1622 Folsom St.
San Francisco, CA 94103
Phone: 415-621-5661
Fax: 415-621-5466

http://www.juvjustice.org

Web site for **Coalition for Juvenile Justice**, which provides information on preventing delinquency as well as current issues in ju-

venile justice. This site provides resources for those working with juveniles and the public and a link to information on the juvenile court system that is jargon free.

Mailing Address:
1710 Rhode Island Ave. NW, 10th Floor
Washington, DC 20036
Phone: 202-467-0864
Fax: 202-887-0738
E-mail: info@juvjustice.org

http://www.fbi.gov/homepage.htm

Website for the **FBI**. Contains a wealth of information on crime and delinquency and, perhaps most important, *Uniform Crime Reports* (*UCR*) data on arrests in the United States.

Mailing Address:
Federal Bureau of Investigation
J. Edgar Hoover Building
935 Pennsylvania Ave. NW
Washington, DC 20535-0001

http://www.usdoj.gov/kidspage/

Web site for **Justice for Kids and Youth.** Provides resources for teachers, parents, and children on crime prevention, drug education, and civil rights. There are also links for children to discuss cyberethics and why it is unethical to commit computer crimes.

Mailing Address:
U.S. Department of Justice
950 Pennsylvania Ave. NW
Washington, DC 20530-0001
Phone: 202-353-1555
E-mail: AskDOJ@usdoj.gov

http://www.jrsainfo.org/

Web site for the **Justice Research and Statistics Association** (JRSA), a national nonprofit organization dedicated to providing information and technical assistance on issues related to the criminal justice system in the United States. Data are presented by state, so this site is useful when doing comparative research.

Mailing Address:
Justice Research and Statistics Association
777 North Capitol St. NE, Suite 801
Washington, DC 20002
Phone: 202-842-9330
Fax: 202-842-9329
E-mail: cjinfo@jrsa.org

http://www.juvenilenet.org

Web site for **Juvenile Information Network**, which provides information on crime prevention and other issues affecting juvenile justice, such as the death penalty and truancy. Conference materials are archived on this site for researchers and students, along with links for families that provide contact information for community services and organizations.
E-mail: webmaster@juvenilenet.org

http://www.monitoringthefuture.org

Web site for **Monitoring the Future**, an organization that annually surveys children from grade school to college to assess their behaviors, attitudes, and values. This site contains many links to articles regarding youth and drug use.
Mailing Address:
Institute for Social Research
University of Michigan
P.O. Box 1248
426 Thompson St.
Ann Arbor, MI 48106-1248
Phone: 734-764-8354
E-mail: MTFinfo@isr.umich.edu

http://ncjj.servehttp.com/NCJJWebsite/main.htm

Web site for the **National Center for Juvenile Justice** (NCJJ), a private, nonprofit resource for independent and original research on topics related directly and indirectly to the field of juvenile justice.
Mailing Address:
710 Fifth Ave., Suite 3000
Pittsburgh, PA 15219

Phone: 412-227-6950
Fax: 412-227-6955

http://www.ncjrs.org

Web site for the **National Criminal Justice Reference Service.** This site provides a database where one can search for abstracts or full text publications on a wide variety of criminal justice issues. There are also links for grants and funding.

Mailing Address:
P.O. Box 6000
Rockville, MD 20849-6000
Phone: 800-851-3420
Fax: 301-519-5212

http://www.iir.com/nygc/

Web site for the **National Youth Gang Center**, which provides information on gangs, research conducted on gangs, and federal and state policies directed at gangs. There also is a link to frequently asked questions regarding gangs, as well as information on conferences and training.

Mailing Address:
Institute for Intergovernmental Research
P.O. Box 12729
Tallahassee, FL 32317
Phone: 850-385-0600
Fax: 850-386-5356
E-mail: nygc@iir.com

http://ojjdp.ncjrs.org/

Web site for the **Office of Juvenile Justice and Delinquency Prevention** (OJJDP). A valuable resource for information on delinquency and the juvenile justice system in the United States. This is an excellent Web site to visit first as you begin your research.

Mailing Address:
OJJDP
810 Seventh St. NW
Washington, DC 20531
Phone: 202-307-5911

Fax: 202-307-2093
E-mail: Askjj@ncjrs.org

http://oas.samhsa.gov/nhsda.htm

Web site for the **Substance Abuse and Mental Health Services Administration** (SAMHSA). The SAMHSA conducts the National Survey on Drug Use and Health annually. This site provides links to reports discussing drug use among youth, as well as treatment.

Mailing Address:
5600 Fishers Lane
Room 12 –105 Parklawn Building
Rockville, MD 20857
Phone: 301-443-4795
Fax: 301-443-0284

http://www.ncjrs.org/txtfiles/fs000202.txt

Link to a document titled "**Trends in Juvenile Violence in European Countries.**"

http://www.unhchr.ch/html/menu3/b/h_comp47.htm

Web site for the **United Nations Guidelines for the Prevention of Juvenile Delinquency**, which includes information on general prevention, socialization, and legislation, along with research and policy development.

Mailing Address:
Office of the High Commissioner for Human Rights
United Nations Office at Geneva
1211 Geneva 10, Switzerland
E-mail: 1503@ohchr.org

Films That Address Juvenile Delinquency and the Juvenile Justice System

Blood Brothers: The Derek and Alex King Case

This video is part of A&E Television's series *American Justice* and is fifty minutes in length. *Blood Brothers* examines the brutal murder of forty-year-old Terry King and the confessions of his two young sons Derek and Alex King, as well as the role of convicted child molester and family friend Rick Chavis. Prosecutor David Rimmer follows the trials of the two boys and Chavis for first-degree murder and examines what may have led these two young boys to kill their own father.

Bullied to Death

This video is part of A&E Television's series *American Justice* and is fifty minutes in length. This film looks at the problem of school-yard bullying and its possible devastating effects. *Bullied to Death* focuses on one case in which a child who was bullied takes his own life and on the Columbine school shooting, in which two students who were bullied released their own pain through violence.

Columbine: Investigating Why

This video is part of A&E Television's series *Investigative Reports* and is fifty minutes in length. A threat assessment group made up of forensic scientist Park Dietz discusses how forensic science tools are used to better understand the mental state of the offenders at Columbine. The group discusses how there were many variables that came together to create this tragedy.

Inside Story: Kids Behind Bars

This fifty-minute video produced by A&E Television examines the policy of juvenile transfer and the dangers associated with placing children in adult prisons and jails with adult sentences. Interviews are conducted with delinquent offenders, criminologists, judges, police, and corrections officers to better understand the social impact of this policy.

The Jonesboro Schoolyard Ambush

This video is part of A&E Television's series *American Justice*. The fifty-minute film examines the 1998 Jonesboro school shootings. This crime was planned and executed by two middle school boys, eleven and thirteen years old. Interviews with experts examine the warning signs, what could be done in the future to prevent such a tragedy, as well as the changes in the Arkansas juvenile justice system in response to this crime. Family members of the offenders are also interviewed to better understand the boys' lives and experiences.

Juvenile Justice

This film is an episode from the PBS show *Front Line* that aired on January 30, 2001. This video is ninety minutes long and examines the issue of juvenile transfer to adult court for serious violent crimes. This episode tracks four juvenile offenders through the juvenile justice system in Santa Clara, California, studying how the four cases are handled.

Juvenile Justice

This video is part of A&E Television's series *American Justice* and is fifty minutes long. This film looks at serious violent crime committed by juveniles and specifically looks at cases that have been in the news. Interviews were conducted with those who worked on these cases, and a discussion is included on how the juvenile justice system has changed to handle these serious offenders.

Juvies

This video is part of A&E Television's series *Investigative Reports* and is 100 minutes in length. The stories of four juvenile offenders in Maryland's Cheltenham Youth Facility are the subject of this film, along with their tragedies and triumphs as they move through the juvenile justice system that focuses upon treatment instead of rehabilitation.

The Killer at Thurston High

This is an episode from the PBS show *Front Line* that aired on January 18, 2000. This episode is ninety minutes in length and looks at the story of fifteen-year-old Kip Kinkel, who murdered his parents and then went on to school, where he shot and wounded twenty-five people and murdered two fellow students.

Listening to Children: A Moral Journey with Robert Coles

This video was produced by PBS and is ninety minutes long. Child psychiatrist Robert Coles examines how children learn values and the difference between right and wrong. Coles studies eight children who are struggling with problems ranging from families falling apart to AIDS.

Little Criminals

This is an episode from the PBS show *Front Line* that aired on May 13, 1997. This sixty-minute film examines the case of a six-year-old California boy who, while trying to steal a tricycle, nearly beat to death a thirty-day-old infant. The six-year-old was the youngest person in the United States to be charged with attempted murder. This episode focuses upon the community where this crime took place to better understand these actions.

The New Face of Crime

This video is part of A&E Television's series *Investigative Reports* and is fifty minutes in length. *The New Face of Crime* looks at how street gangs have evolved into organized and effective criminal networks. This film features interviews with gang members and the police and thus gives us a better understanding of this problem from both perspectives.

The New Skinheads

This video is part of A&E Television's series *Investigative Reports* and is fifty minutes in length. This film studies the skinhead movement and its beginnings in Europe, as well as how the movement has grown and changed. The message of the current skinheads, their involvement with the Ku Klux Klan and other hate groups, and the crimes these youth commit, are examined.

Teen Gambling

Teen Gambling is part of A&E Television's series *Investigative Reports* and is fifty minutes in length. This film looks at gambling in the United States and how the easy availability of gambling has affected teenagers. Interviews are conducted with teenagers whose own addictions caused them to eventually become delinquent and commit crimes, as well as with teachers, parents, and experts.

Teenagers under the Gun

This fifty-minute video is part of A&E Television's series *Investigative Reports*. The video examines at-risk youth and their chances of committing and participating in violent crimes. It includes interviews with children who are at risk for serious delinquency and focuses on their explanations for what might possibly drive them to crime.

When a Child Kills

This video is part of A&E Television's series *American Justice* and is fifty minutes in length. This film examines the case of Nathaniel Abraham, who was eleven years old when he murdered eighteen-year-old Ronnie Green. This film includes interviews with those who worked on Abraham's case and focuses on his arrest and conviction as an adult even though he was an adolescent at the time of the crime and the trial.

Glossary

Boot Camps   Boot camps are a modern version of the "get tough" philosophy as applied to the treatment and prevention of delinquency. The traditional boot camp model is based on a military-style boot camp experience, with harsh discipline and treatment of residents. More recently, however, other models of boot camps have appeared, such as those based on conciliation efforts and educational opportunities instead of, or in addition to, harsh military discipline.

Chicago Area Project (CAP)   This is a community-based, anti-gang and delinquency prevention program begun in Chicago in the 1930s. It has now spread to other cities in Illinois. The CAP involves local community and neighborhood leaders in a joint effort to provide more conventional choices for young people, such as educational and recreational opportunities, as an alternative to the attraction of criminal role models and lifestyles in the community.

Child Savers (Child-Saving Movement)   Child savers were a collection of reformists and philanthropists who worked in the last half of the nineteenth century to change the laws in the country to specifically target delinquency. The first of these laws was created in 1899 in Chicago.

Chronic Few   The so-called chronic few refers to the relatively small percentage of juveniles (perhaps between 6 and 10 percent) who can be classified as serious habitual offenders. This small group is often responsible for most of the serious and violent juvenile crime in a community.

Cohort Study   Cohort studies follow the same group (cohort) of people over a long period of time. The landmark cohort study "Delinquency in a Birth Cohort" was conducted by criminologist Marvin Wolfgang and his colleagues. These studies have revealed that a small percentage of offenders, the so-called chronic few, are responsible for most of the serious and violent crime in a community.

Community Policing   This approach to law enforcement involves the police and members of the community working together to prevent crimes. Its philosophical approach is based on creating a partnership between the police and the community.

Diversion   Diversion involves using noninstitutional programs and procedures for handling juveniles. Some diversion programs start at the point of arrest, while others are used after a youth has appeared in juvenile court. One of the aims of diversion programs is to reduce the stigma of having been identified and handled within the formal system of juvenile justice.

Drug Court   This is a relatively recent concept now being used in both juvenile and adults court systems. A drug court is both a treatment and a punitive response to the problem of drug addiction and drug use, particularly if such behavior involves delinquent or criminal activity. It typically involves a treatment plan of at least twelve months, accompanied by regular visits to court and intensive supervision by a probation officer.

Empirical Study   This refers to scientific research that answers questions (for example, Do males commit more delinquency than females?) by gathering the best available evidence. Such studies need to be done objectively and thoroughly in order to be credible.

Extralegal   This term refers to factors or circumstances that are outside of, or separate from, legal considerations (for example, race, social class, and gender). The juvenile justice and adult criminal justice systems are supposed to make decisions based on legal, not extralegal, factors.

Garden-Variety Delinquency   This term refers to common and less serious forms of delinquent behavior, such as truancy, underage drinking, and vandalism.

House of Refuge   Houses of refuge were established to rehabilitate youthful offenders. They usually housed wayward and vagrant children and were known for operating by strict disciplinarian rules and procedures. They were the forerunners to juvenile correctional institutions. The first house of refuge was created in New York City in 1825.

Index Offenses   There are eight index or Part I criminal offenses measured by the FBI's *Uniform Crime Reports:* murder, rape, robbery, aggravated assault, larceny-theft, motor vehicle theft, burglary, and arson. Together, these eight crimes form the crime index that measures the incidence of serious crime in the United States.

Juvenile Correctional Institutions Correctional institutions for juveniles are considered long-term facilities whose mission is both to control and to rehabilitate youth. These institutions can be either public or private.

Juvenile Delinquent Any minor youth (usually under age eighteen) who commits a crime or a status offense.

Juvenile Gang (or Youth Gang) A juvenile gang is a collection of juveniles, usually between the ages of eleven or twelve and eighteen or nineteen, and usually of the same gender, who band together to engage in collective activities, including criminal behavior. Such gangs usually communicate with their own members and with other gangs through hand signals, clothing styles, and graffiti. Such delinquent groups are difficult to control.

Juvenile Justice and Delinquency Prevention (JJDP) Act This law was passed in 1974 and had an important effect on juvenile justice systems throughout the country. One of the most significant features of the act was that it required states to eliminate or modify their status offense laws. Almost all states have done so in the past thirty years.

Mandatory Minimum Sentences This term refers to the statutory or legal requirement that minimum sentences be applied, regardless of mitigating circumstances, to certain crimes. These sentences are most often applied in drug convictions. Many experts who study criminal justice are highly critical of them.

Massachusetts Experiment This was a deinstitutionalization program initiated in the early 1970s by Jerome Miller. The program at first involved reforms to existing practices in the Massachusetts juvenile correction system but eventually resulted in the closing of almost all juvenile corrections facilities in that state.

MDMA (or Ecstasy) MDMA is methylenedioxymethamphetamine, a powerful and increasingly popular drug among young people. It is sometimes referred to as a club drug or rave drug because it is used at dance parties (raves). Its effects include euphoria and increased self-confidence. Its has serious side effects, including damage to nerve cells, depression, and even death.

Monitoring the Future (MTF) This is an annual self-report survey of U.S. adolescents conducted by researchers at the Institute for Social Research at the University of Michigan. It surveys approximately 45,000 students in an effort to measure their involvement in delinquent behavior.

Multisystemic Therapy (MST)   MST involves a holistic approach to the treatment of delinquency. It includes members of the community, including juveniles' families, law enforcement personnel, the court system, schools, churches, and others who play a vital role in the education and supervision of youth, in a joint effort to reduce and prevent delinquency.

Net Widening   This concept is related to diversion programs. It usually involves more juveniles being brought into the system of juvenile justice, or at least being identified within the system, as a result of diversion programs.

Oregon Social Learning Center (OSLC)   This is a treatment-oriented institution connected with the University of Oregon. The center's method of treating delinquency is to involve family members and to emphasize proper methods of exercising parental discipline and supervision in ways that will help reduce delinquency.

Parens Patriae   *Parens patriae* is a legal concept associated with old English common law. It means that the state is the father of the country and thus has the legal right to do whatever it deems best in the interest of juveniles and of society, including removing misbehaving or abused children from their homes, with or without parental consent.

Restorative Justice   This philosophy emphasizes offender-victim reconciliation, including relatives of both parties in a crime. Details differ, but all restorative programs involve a professional mediator, sometimes a probation officer, who tries to get both sides in a juvenile crime to agree to an acceptable resolution to the crime. In some countries, such as Australia and New Zealand, this concept is coupled with the concept of reintegrative shaming.

Retributive Justice   This philosophy involves punishment or just deserts. When people speak of "an eye for an eye and a tooth for a tooth," they are referring to the concept of retribution.

Self-Report Study   Self-report studies ask a sample of people (typically adolescents) to report their own experiences with law violation. The MTF is an example of a self-report study.

Status Offense   A status offense is an act of illegality, not a crime. It is used for youth under the age of majority, usually eighteen. An example of a status offense is truancy. These laws have become controversial and many have been modified or eliminated by states in the past thirty years.

Therapeutic Community   This treatment concept attempts to create a more integrated approach to the rehabilitation of delinquents and criminals. Often, therapeutic communities are found in group homes or halfway houses, places where offenders are housed after spending time in an institution.

Uniform Crime Reports (UCR)   An annual publication produced by the FBI on crimes and arrests in the country. While most of the data in the *UCR* involve crimes, some status offenses are also included, such as running away from home.

Victim Survey   Victim surveys ask a sample of people to report their experiences as victims of crime and delinquency. The most well-known and important victim survey is the National Crime Victimization Survey (NCVS), which is conducted annually in the United States.

Waiver (or Transfer)   Waiver means to transfer a case from juvenile court to the adult criminal justice system. Youth whose cases are waived are treated as adults and are thus subjected to the death penalty (if they were at least sixteen years old at the time the crime was committed).

Index

About the Authors

Donald J. Shoemaker received a Ph.D. in sociology in 1970 and is currently Professor of Sociology at Virginia Tech. He has published extensively in the field of crime and delinquency, including a fifth edition of *Theories of Delinquency* published by Oxford University Press. Professor Shoemaker has also conducted international research on crime and delinquency, particularly in the Philippines, and has written several articles on crime and delinquency in the Philippines. Current research interests include evaluation research and studies of violent crime and delinquency.

Timothy W. Wolfe, Ph.D., is Associate Professor and Department Chair of Sociology at Mount Saint Mary's University in Emmitsburg, Maryland. His research on delinquency and theory integration has appeared in the *American Journal of Criminal Justice* and the *Quarterly Journal of Ideology*. His research on college student binge drinking has appeared in *Sociological Spectrum*, the *College Student Journal*, and the *Journal of Alcohol and Drug Education*. He currently resides in Taneytown, Maryland, with his wife, Doria, and their four sons: Tim, Jr., Matt, Joe, and James. When not teaching or writing, he loves to play jazz saxophone.